W9-BMZ-775

THESE BLACK LINES
APPEAR TO BEND AWAY
FROM THE CENTER OF
THE BLUE LINES. BUT
DO THEY REALLY?

FIND OUT ON PAGE 19

NATIONAL GEOGRAPHIC KiDS

BRAIN GAMES

BIG BOOK OF BOREDOM BUSTERS

STEPHANIE WARREN DRIMMER
AND DR. GARETH MOORE

NATIONAL GEOGRAPHIC
WASHINGTON, D.C.

CONTENTS

CHAPTER ONE:
CALLING ALL GENIUSES [6]
OPERATING INSTRUCTIONS [8]
BUDDY SYSTEM [10]

CHAPTER TWO:
THE SENSES [12]
VISION: OUR DOMINANT SENSE [14]
PUZZLES & GAMES [16]

CHAPTER THREE:
WORDS AND LANGUAGE [34]
HEAR YE, HEAR YE! [36]
PUZZLES & GAMES [38]

CHAPTER FOUR:
SPATIAL SMARTS [56]
MENTAL MAPMAKING [58]
PUZZLES & GAMES [60]

CHAPTER FIVE:
PROBLEM SOLVING [78]
LOGICAL LEARNING [80]
PUZZLES & GAMES [82]

CHAPTER SIX:
BRAIN MYSTERIES [100]
YOUR HIDDEN BRAIN [102]
PUZZLES & GAMES [104]

CHAPTER SEVEN:
ANIMAL INTELLIGENCE [122]
CRAFTY CREATURES [124]
PUZZLES & GAMES [126]

ANSWERS [144]
INDEX [156]
CREDITS [160]

CALLING ALL GENIUSES

DID YOU KNOW THAT YOU ALREADY HAVE IN YOUR POSSESSION THE MOST POWERFUL SUPERCOMPUTER IN THE UNIVERSE?

Nope, it's not your laptop or a gaming system or any other device. It's a wrinkly, squishy pink thing about the size of a softball: your brain.

Your brain may be small, but it's mighty. It controls how you talk and think, what you remember, and how you move. Your brain is what makes you who you are. And yet, much of how the brain works is a mystery. Scientists know more about stars exploding billions of light-years away than they do about the human brain!

Why? Well ... believe it or not, your noggin is the most complex structure in the known universe. Right now, your brain is moving your eyes across this page, converting the squiggles you see into words you can understand, and comprehending the meaning of those words. Your brain is hard at work every second of the day—and even at night while you're sleeping.

And because your brain does so much, it never hurts to give it a bit of a boost. This book is jam-packed with puzzles designed to give you a mental workout *and* bring the fun. (Some are harder than others, so if you find yourself a little stumped, move on to the next one or ask a friend for help!) Along the way, you'll also learn more about how your magnificent mind does what it does. So, are you ready to find out what your amazing brain can do?

LET THE GAMES BEGIN! $\longrightarrow$

OPERATING INSTRUCTIONS

BEFORE YOU GEAR UP TO BECOME A PUZZLE-SOLVING MACHINE, LET'S GO OVER SOME OF THE BASICS OF BRAIN SCIENCE.

NERVE NETWORK

Your brain is connected to a network of nerve cells, or neurons, that extends throughout your body. You have more than 86 billion neurons! They're all linked together, making trillions of connections. Your neurons are how your brain communicates with your body. Bits of information zip around your neuron network at 150 miles an hour (241 km/h)—about twice as fast as a car speeds down the highway!

This system runs on the power of electricity. When a neuron is getting ready to send a signal, it gains a small electric charge. That triggers the neuron next to it to become charged, and then the next. Signals travel by jumping from neuron to neuron all the way from your head to your toes. Your brain produces enough electricity to power a lightbulb!

MIND MAP

The largest part of your brain, the cerebrum, controls all your thoughts and actions. It's divided into different areas, or lobes, each with its own job.

Parietal lobe: Your parietal lobe processes information from your senses of taste, temperature, and touch. When you pick up an ice cube, the parietal lobe processes its slick surface and cold temperature.

Occipital lobe: Have you ever admired a beautiful sunset? Thank your occipital lobe, which processes visual images.

Temporal lobe: Without your temporal lobe, you wouldn't be able to understand someone talking to you. This area helps process language and sound, as well as smell, taste, and memory.

Frontal lobe: The frontal lobe has maybe the most important job of all: It makes plans and decisions, and it organizes your thoughts. The frontal lobe controls reasoning and problem solving.

YOU HAVE **NEURONS** THAT STRETCH FROM THE BOTTOM OF YOUR **SPINE** TO YOUR **BIG TOE.**

THERE ARE AS MANY **NEURONS** IN YOUR **BRAIN** AS THERE ARE **STARS** IN THE **MILKY WAY.**

FRONTAL LOBE

PARIETAL LOBE

TEMPORAL LOBE

OCCIPITAL LOBE

→BUDDY SYSTEM

YOUR BRAIN IS DIVIDED INTO TWO HALVES. EACH SIDE OF THE BRAIN CONTROLS THE OPPOSITE SIDE OF YOUR BODY. WHEN YOU MOVE YOUR LEFT HAND, THAT ACTION IS CONTROLLED BY THE RIGHT SIDE OF YOUR BRAIN. WHEN YOU WINK YOUR RIGHT EYE, IT'S THE LEFT SIDE OF YOUR BRAIN THAT'S RESPONSIBLE.

The two sides, the right brain and the left brain, are connected by a bridge of nerve fibers called the corpus callosum. Each side has its own special set of skills. In most people, the left side of the brain is better at tasks involving logic and rational thinking. The right side usually handles more creative and emotional tasks.

But it's a myth that some people are "right-brained" and others "left-brained." Different sides of the brain might have different strengths, but they have to work together to accomplish tasks. For example, studies have shown that the left side of the brain is better at some math-related jobs like counting and reciting the multiplication tables. But the right side of the brain is better at other math tasks, like estimating how many of something there are. To be good at math—or writing, art, or anything else—you need both sides of your head to work together.

STUDYING THE BRAIN

How do we know what's going on inside someone's head? Here are a few of the tools scientists use to sneak a peek inside the brain.

Electricity Detectors

Your brain runs on electricity that can be detected and recorded. In EEG (electroencephalography), small metal discs attached to the scalp sense those signals, and then a computer converts them into a pattern. Other times, very thin wires called electrodes are put inside the brain itself to detect the activity of a few neurons at a time.

CT

A CT (computed tomography) scanner takes a series of x-rays and puts them together to create a three-dimensional image of the brain. CT scans show only what the brain looks like, not how it works.

EVER WONDER WHY YOUR BRAIN IS **WRINKLED?** THE FOLDS INCREASE SURFACE AREA, MAKING MORE SPACE FOR NERVE CELLS TO BE PACKED IN. WRINKLES EQUAL **WISDOM.**

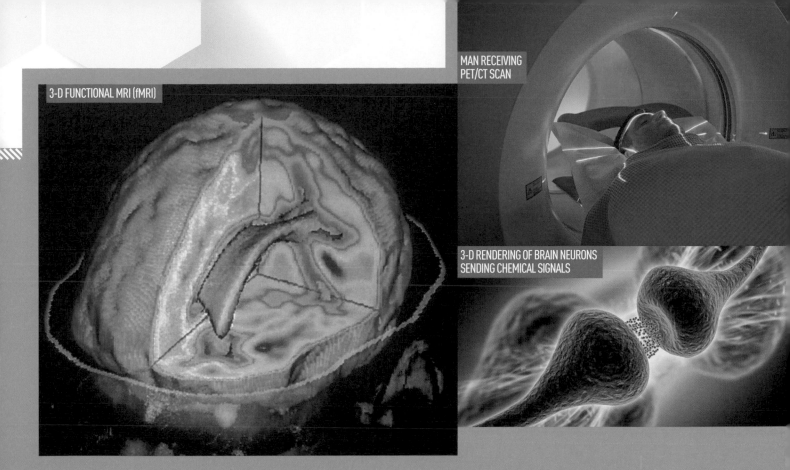

3-D FUNCTIONAL MRI (fMRI)

MAN RECEIVING PET/CT SCAN

3-D RENDERING OF BRAIN NEURONS SENDING CHEMICAL SIGNALS

MRI

In MRI (magnetic resonance imaging), a huge magnet moves around the patient, creating a magnetic field. Then soundless radio waves are aimed at the patient's brain. The brain's atoms respond by sending out their own waves, which a computer can measure and turn into a picture.

fMRI

A functional MRI (or fMRI) goes one step beyond an MRI: It takes pictures of blood flowing through the brain, showing brain activity.

MEG

An MEG (magnetoencephalography) scanner is cooled to 500 degrees below freezing (-296°C), so cold that the machine's atoms are barely moving. That allows the machine to detect the movement of the brain's atoms. MEG is the best way to see the brain in action, but for now, the machines are very expensive and most hospitals don't have one.

YOUR BRAIN IS **77** PERCENT WATER.

ACCIDENTS AND INJURIES

Before modern medicine, a lot of what doctors knew about the brain came from examining people who had brain injuries. In 1848, a man named Phineas Gage was working on a railroad when an explosion sent a four-foot (1.2-m)-long iron pole through his head. Amazingly, Gage survived, but people who knew him before and after the accident observed that his personality had changed as a result: He had gone, they said, from a reasonable, likable man to a rude, unpleasant one. The doctor who had treated Gage, John Harlow, examined the railroad foreman's skull after his death and believed that the iron rod had damaged the part of Gage's brain that controls personality. Behavior, scientists would later find, is indeed tied to different areas of the brain.

CHAPTER TWO

THE SENSES

What are you sensing right now? You probably aren't giving it too much thought. But if you focus, you might be feeling the pages of this book under your fingers, hearing the sound of cars outside your window, and smelling dinner cooking in the kitchen.

Your senses—touch, taste, smell, hearing, and vision—are how you interact with the world around you. All of them work by taking in information and converting it to electrical signals, the language of the brain.

VANISHING COLORS

THERE ARE FIVE COLOR CIRCLES ON THIS PAGE, all on a pink background. Believe it or not, you can make them vanish just by looking at them! Hold the book close to you and keep it still, and then focus on the center of the yellow circle and try not to move your eyes or blink. As you watch, the red, dark blue, light blue, and green circles vanish, and then the yellow circle fades out, too. Last of all, the pink fades to gray—and you are left with a blank page!

[BEHIND THE BRAIN]

What's going on here?!? The colors appear to fade because you are keeping your eyes still. When your eyes start to get tired, they stop telling your brain about the bits that haven't changed. So, over a small amount of time, they appear to fade from view. Amazing!

→ VISION: OUR DOMINANT SENSE

ALMOST ONE-THIRD OF YOUR BRAIN IS DEVOTED TO PROCESSING INFORMATION FROM YOUR EYES. FOR MOST PEOPLE, IT'S THE MAIN WAY WE TAKE IN THE WORLD AROUND US. HERE'S HOW IT WORKS:

→ Light enters your eye through the pupil.

→ It passes through your lens, which changes shape to focus the image on the back of your eye.

→There, light-sensitive cells respond by creating electrical signals that travel down your optic nerves to your brain. These electrical signals are like a code that your brain can read to make sense of what your eyes are seeing.

HIDDEN SENSES

If you were asked to name the senses, you'd probably have no trouble listing five. But did you know that you have lots of other senses, too?

There's proprioception, the awareness of where your body parts are; you use it when you touch a finger to your nose. There's nociception, the sense of pain, which lets you know when you stub a toe. Then there's temporal perception, which helps you sense time. And these are just a few—depending on which brain scientist you ask, humans have 10, a dozen, or even hundreds of senses!

ILLUSTRATION SHOWING THE VISUAL PATHWAYS FROM THE RETINAS OF THE EYES TO THE BRAIN'S CEREBRAL CORTEX

VISUAL LIMITS

We see our world in three dimensions. Without 3-D vision, we couldn't even cross the street safely. But guess what? Your eyes can't actually see in 3-D. The information they take in and send to your brain is only in 2-D, like a painting. Your brain has to figure out depth all by itself. It combines images from both eyes, using clues

like highlights and shadows around an object to fill in the picture.

Here's another eye-opener: At the back of each eyeball, there's a spot where your optic nerve attaches to the eyes. This area can't detect light—it's a blind spot. Try the puzzle called "Blind Spot" on page 23 to find yours!

TRICKING THE MIND

In the pages ahead, you'll see puzzles that will make you think your eyes are playing tricks on you. They're called optical illusions, pictures that use light, color, or patterns to fool the brain into seeing something that isn't there. But how can this happen?

Your brain takes in a constant barrage of information from your senses. To process all that in real time, it has to take shortcuts. It uses information it already knows about how the world works to make educated guesses. It usually gets things right ... but not always—and optical illusions and other puzzles that fool your senses show that in action. Don't believe it? Turn the page and see for yourself!

THE
HUMAN
BRAIN,
ON AVERAGE, PROCESSES
TENS OF
THOUSANDS
OF THOUGHTS
A DAY.

IMAGE COMBINATION ANSWERS PAGE 144

IMAGINE COMBINING THESE TWO IMAGES so that the white squares on one image are replaced with the contents of the color squares from the other. Can you answer these questions about the resulting picture?

How many **blue** hexagons are there?

ANSWER →

How many **red** circles are partially overlapped by **blue** hexagons?

ANSWER →

How many **red** circles do not overlap with any other shape?

ANSWER →

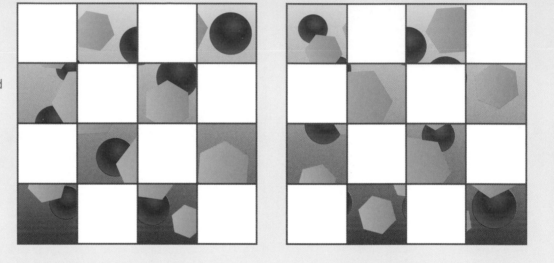

IMAGE STACKING ANSWERS PAGE 144

FOUR TILES, numbered **1 to 4,** have been stacked in each of the pictures labeled **A** and **B.**

If you know that none of the tiles have been rotated, can you figure out the exact order they were stacked in to make each of the two pictures?

ANSWER →

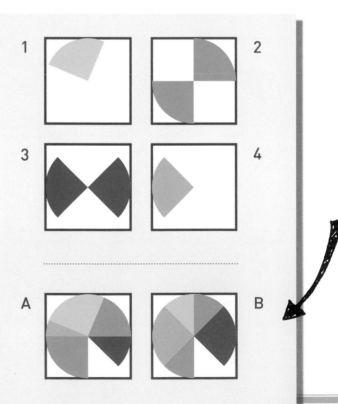

HIDDEN SHAPES

ANSWERS PAGE 144

CAN YOU FIND THIS FOUR-POINTED STAR
HIDDEN SOMEWHERE AMONG ALL THE LINES?
It may be a different size or may have been rotated,
but other than that it will be exactly the same. It's
surprisingly tricky to find, so congratulations
if you find it quickly!

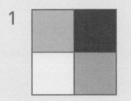

HIDDEN PATTERNS

ANSWERS PAGE 144

HOW QUICKLY CAN YOU LOCATE EACH OF THESE
PATTERNS, numbered 1 and 2, in the grid below
them? Unlike in the previous puzzle, they can't
be rotated—so what you are looking for is
exactly what you see.

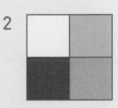

PARALLEL LINES

THESE ZIPPER-LIKE RED AND BLUE LINES APPEAR TO RUN UP THE PAGE AT DIFFERENT ANGLES—but it's just an illusion! They are, in fact, perfectly parallel and are all at the same angle to one another. Place a ruler over the page to test this out!

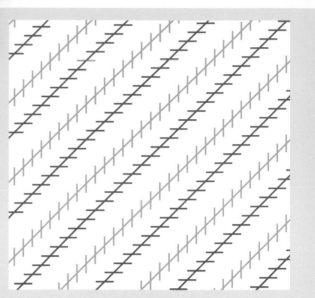

HIDDEN

SQUARE ANSWERS PAGE 144

AT FIRST GLANCE, THIS APPEARS TO BE A SIMPLE REPEATING PATTERN, but hidden within it is a square that differs from the rest. At normal reading distance it isn't immediately obvious, though you will probably find it if you look for it. Instead, try putting the book down so that you can see this page, and then step back quite some way away. The border of the square that's different should be much more obvious!

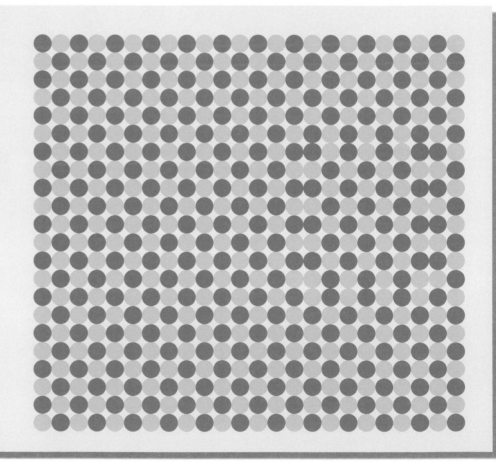

STRAIGHT LINES

THESE BLACK LINES APPEAR TO BEND AWAY from the center of the blue lines. But do they really? Use a ruler or another straight-edged object to check!

[BEHIND THE BRAIN]

There are various possible explanations for this illusion, but one explanation is that the radial blue lines give the impression to the eye that the picture represents a 3-D image where the center is far away. It then corrects for this perception of depth, curving the black lines to correct for their relative positions compared to the blue lines. This is called the Hering illusion.

SQUARE DOTS

ANSWERS PAGE 144

THIS APPEARS TO BE A CIRCLE OF DOTS, but if you join them up in the correct way you can also make a square! By drawing just four straight lines that pass through the centers of the dots, can you form a perfect square? Every dot must be used, but the square can be at any angle.

WHITE BALANCE CORRECTION

BOOM!

WHAT DO YOU THINK IS THE COLOR OF THE CENTER TILE IN EACH OF THESE FOUR PICTURES?

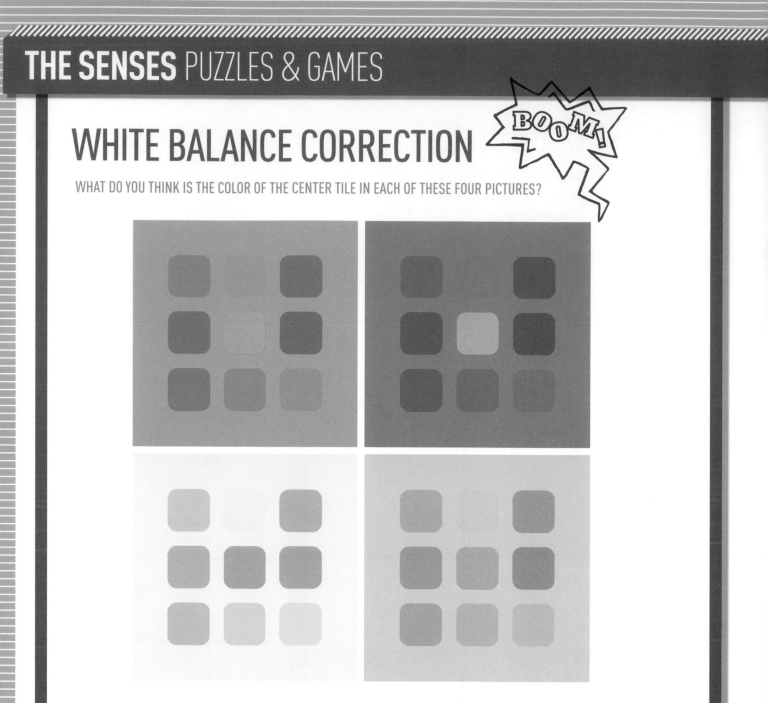

Simple, right? The top-left center tile appears to be green, the top-right one yellow, the bottom-left blue, and the bottom-right purple. But is this really correct? Nope! Can you believe that each center tile is really the exact same gray color shown in the center tile here? Grab a piece of scrap paper and place it over the page, then make four small holes so you can see each gray tile without the surrounding colors. Now you can see that they really are all the same color!

[BEHIND THE BRAIN]

The large color squares overlaid on top of each set of nine tiles trick your eye into thinking that there is a colored light shining on each set of tiles. Your brain then corrects for this, resulting in differently colored center tiles—even though they are all the same gray. And why do you see a blue tile for a yellow light, or a purple tile for a green light? It's because these are complementary colors, which means that if you combine the light of these two colors, you'll end up with a colorless white or gray light.

LIGHTBULB INVERSION

STARE AT THE CENTER OF THIS COLORFUL LIGHTBULB FOR 20 SECONDS, and then look away at a blank wall surface—ideally, one that isn't too far away so that your eyes don't refocus too much at the same time. You should see a brightly shining lightbulb! If the illusion doesn't work, practice looking away at the wall without having your eyes hunt to focus—and then try again.

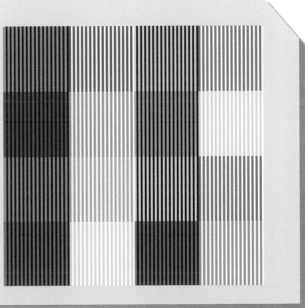

[BEHIND THE BRAIN]

The cones in your eye start to get tired from staring at the same color for a while, so they begin to lose sensitivity; this is the same effect you saw in the puzzle on page 13. When you then look at a plain surface, you see the aftereffect of this—the brain continues to adapt for the loss of sensitivity. This means that you see the negative of each color; the negative of blue light is yellow light, resulting in a glowing bulb.

COLOR PATTERNS ANSWERS PAGE 144

THIS GRID CONTAINS THREE BOXES IN A ROW THAT ARE ALL THE SAME COLOR. The three boxes can run horizontally, vertically, or diagonally. Can you find them? Ignore the white and black lines that run over the top of the grid—they are there to distract you!

PARTIALLY OBSCURED LINE

YESSS!!!

ANSWERS PAGE 144

IMAGINE THAT THE BLUE LINE ON THE LEFT CONTINUES ALL THE WAY TO THE RIGHT OF THE GREEN RECTANGLE. Which of the five blue lines on the right do you think it would match up with?

IMAGINARY CIRCLES

THIS GRID APPEARS TO BE FULL OF PERFECT WHITE CIRCLES. But is it really? Take a closer look—are the circles really there?

[BEHIND THE BRAIN]

This illusion happens because your brain interprets the missing parts of the blue lines as indicating the presence of a hidden object in front of the lines. Without any further information, it makes a sensible guess that the hidden object will cover a roughly circular shape. Scientists think the brain evolved this ability to spot hidden objects—like a camouflaged predator ready to pounce! This is called the Ehrenstein illusion.

BLIND SPOT

HOLD THE BOOK AS FAR AWAY FROM YOU AS YOU CAN, SO THAT YOU CAN CLEARLY SEE ALL THREE BOXES IN THE IMAGE BELOW, and then close your right eye.

Now, keeping your right eye shut, focus on the red box. You should be able to see both the blue and green boxes at the edge of your vision—if you can't, then you need to hold the book farther away, so you might need to prop it up or get someone else to help.

Next, slowly and steadily move the book toward you. As it gets closer, first the blue box vanishes—and then, as it gets even closer, the blue box reappears and the green box vanishes! And then the green box also reappears.

[BEHIND THE BRAIN]

This amazing effect happens because there is a blind spot in each eye where a clump of nerve endings called the optic nerve are attached. These send the information from the eye into the rest of the brain. Normally, you aren't aware of this because the brain fills in the missing bits of the picture with information from your other eye, as well as guesses about the rest of the scene. But when there is an isolated object that isn't visible from either eye, it will simply vanish, as you've just seen.

CIRCULAR ARCS ANSWERS PAGE 144

IN THIS PICTURE YOU CAN SEE THE TOP PART OF THREE DIFFERENT CIRCLES. Which of the circles do you think is the largest and which is the smallest ... or are any the same size?

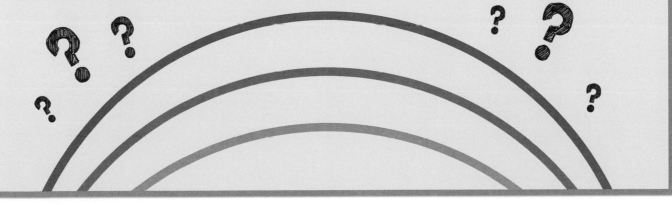

CENTER OF TRIANGLE
ANSWERS PAGE 145

THIS TRIANGULAR WIZARD'S HAT HAS TWO STARS ON IT.
Which of these stars do you think is in the exact vertical center of the hat, measured vertically straight down from the point at the top?

CIRCLE SQUARES
ANSWERS PAGE 145

WHICH OF THESE TWO CENTRAL ORANGE SQUARES LOOKS TO BE THE LARGER ONE?

MATCHING RECTANGLE
ANSWERS PAGE 145

THE PICTURE BELOW SHOWS THREE HORIZONTAL RECTANGLES STACKED BELOW A GREEN VERTICAL RECTANGLE. The green vertical is exactly the same size as one of the other rectangles—but which one?

SIDE BY SIDE

THE PATH ON THE LEFT OF THIS PICTURE APPEARS TO LEAN MUCH MORE STRONGLY TO THE LEFT THAN THE PATH ON THE RIGHT DOES. But does it really? Using a protractor or a ruler, measure the angle of each path to find out.

[BEHIND THE BRAIN]

The two paths lean at exactly the same angle. Your brain, however, interprets the two paths as belonging to a single 3-D scene, with just one, mutual vanishing point in the distance. Given this information, it knows that the paths must lead away at different angles in order to appear the same, so it essentially corrects for reality.

SLIDING CHECKERS ANSWERS PAGE 145

IT'S TIME TO MAKE YOUR OWN OPTICAL ILLUSION! Grab your coloring pencils and color each of the empty squares the same light color, such as yellow or pale green, and then color all the dotted squares the same dark color, such as dark blue, brown, or even black. What do you see now?

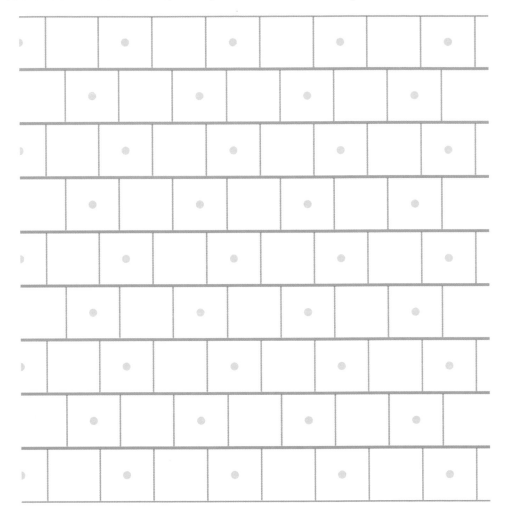

In the resulting image, you should see two different illusions:
- The horizontal lines now appear to angle slightly up and down.
- If you run your eyes quickly around the image, the tiles appear to move slightly from side to side.

[BEHIND THE BRAIN]

The angled lines appear because your brain interprets the misaligned colored blocks as evidence that the rows of squares tilt. If you see the sliding blocks, this is because your brain assumes that they should be lined up, and so it tries to correct for how it thinks they should appear! Your brain does correct for what it's seeing all the time, which is why you can recognize faces even when they're partially obscured—your brain figures out what "must" be there, even though you aren't directly seeing it.

SURROUNDING CONTRAST

like

THE WHITE DIAMONDS IN THE CENTER OF THESE TWO IMAGES BOTH APPEAR TO GLOW much brighter and whiter than the white paper around them. But the paper and the diamonds are exactly the same brightness!

[BEHIND THE BRAIN]

Your brain applies a real-world interpretation to the shaded black rectangles, assuming that the explanation for them fading to white as they near the diamond must be because they are being exposed to a really bright light source. So you see that light shining, even though it isn't really there! In the right-hand picture, the illusion is even stronger because the diamond shape is surrounded by even more shaded black rectangles—the apparently brightly lit elements.

FLOATING SURFACE

DOES THE YELLOW BOX IN THE CENTER OF THIS IMAGE APPEAR TO FLOAT UP ABOVE THE BLUE CIRCLES BELOW? It almost looks like it is floating above the page and that the blue circles are back below the page!

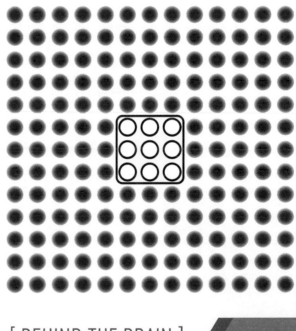

[BEHIND THE BRAIN]

Of course everything is printed on the page (nothing is floating!). Your brain just assumes that the blurred shapes must be in the distance and that the sharp, clearly outlined yellow box must be much closer.

TOUCH PUZZLE

FOR THIS GAME YOU WILL NEED A FRIEND OR SOME OTHER PERSON WHO IS WILLING TO HELP YOU. Offer to swap with them once you've tried it, so they can have a turn, too! Start by having the friend find as many different-sized coins as they can and then place them on a table in front of you. Once you've memorized which coins there are, close your eyes. Now ask your friend to remove one of the coins and rearrange the remaining coins on the table. Finally, without opening your eyes, use just your hands and your sense of touch to figure out which coin is missing.

[BEHIND THE BRAIN]

Did you get it correct? When you feel for a coin, and estimate its size using just the pressure on your fingers, you're using your sense of touch. If you were blind, your sense of touch would become much more sensitive in order to help compensate for your loss of vision, which is how blind people are able to read braille—letters that are written with just raised dots. If you ever try reading braille without any practice, it seems like it would be impossible to ever learn!

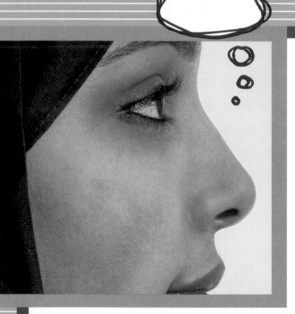

SMELL PUZZLE

YOU'LL NEED A FRIEND FOR THIS ONE, TOO. In fact, you'll need one for all the puzzles on this and the following three pages—so ask them to stick around for a few minutes!

Have your friend find a few different foods with distinctive smells, such as an herb, a banana, or a piece of cheese (or even strongly smelling drinks such as coffee) and to do so without showing you what they are.

Now, close your eyes and ask your friend to hold each object near your nose so that you can sniff it. How many can you correctly identify? Make sure your friend doesn't let you sniff anything that isn't safe to sniff and that you keep your head still so you don't accidentally collide with the item you're sniffing!

[BEHIND THE BRAIN]

Your nose works by detecting microscopic molecules that are released by objects all around us. These land on special detectors in the nose, which link back into your brain. Your smell is in fact an important part of your perception of taste, which is why when your nose is blocked up due to a cold or allergies, you sometimes find that food tastes unusually bland!

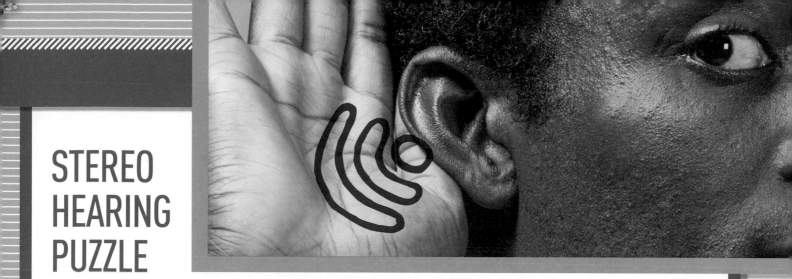

STEREO HEARING PUZZLE

CLOSE YOUR EYES AND HAVE YOUR FRIEND MOVE AS QUIETLY AS THEY CAN TO A NEW LOCATION IN THE SAME ROOM. Then have them say "Hello" to you. Can you work out where they are? Point at them, still with your eyes closed, and then open your eyes to see if you were correct.

Now try the same game again, but this time hold your hand tightly over one of your ears while your friend moves around the room and then says "Hello." Was it harder this time?

[BEHIND THE BRAIN]

There's a very good reason why you have two ears: so your brain can work out where sounds are coming from relative to you. It does this by measuring both the difference in time between a sound arriving at one ear and then arriving at the other, and also by the difference in volume. Using this information, your brain can do a very good job of working out where a sound is coming from, even without using information from your eyes or other senses.

You might also wonder how your brain can tell if sounds are coming from in front of you or behind you. This remarkable ability relies on the shape of your ears, which means that sounds coming from in front of you sound different from sounds coming from behind you—incredible!

TASTE PUZZLE

THIS IS AN ACTIVITY FOR WHICH IT IS BEST TO ASK A PARENT OR GUARDIAN FOR HELP, rather than a friend. Ask them to find a few different foods that are safe to eat, and then ask them to cut a few small cubes of each food. For example, they could cut a few small pieces of an apple, a carrot, a cookie, or some breakfast cereal. The smaller they cut them the better, so you can't easily identify the items just by their texture or shape.

Close your eyes before you have a chance to see any of the foods, and then have them feed you the pieces of each type of food. This is most easily done by placing them on a teaspoon. Now, using just your sense of taste, see if you can identify what you are eating without looking. Some people will find this much easier than others!

[BEHIND THE BRAIN]

Your tongue can detect only a very limited number of distinct types of taste, but by combining information from these different tastes, plus aromas detected by your nose, you are able to both sense and appreciate a wide range of flavors.

TIME PUZZLE

FOR THIS ACTIVITY YOU'LL NEED BOTH A WILLING FRIEND AS WELL AS A WATCH, PHONE, OR OTHER DEVICE THAT CAN ACT AS A STOPWATCH.

The aim of this puzzle is to see how accurately you can estimate the length of a minute. Ask your friend to say "Start" to you when they begin timing you, and from this point on, using only your own judgment—and not by looking at any clock or other timer—call out "Stop!" when you think exactly a minute has passed.

Your friend can then let you know how much time has actually passed, and you can see how close to a minute you were. You might want to try two or three times to see if you get better with practice. And, if a minute is too easy, try two minutes or even three minutes!

[BEHIND THE BRAIN]

You might have been taught that you have five senses, but the fact is that you actually have several more senses than those! One of these is your sense of time. Without it you would have trouble sleeping a full night and would have no idea at all—without checking a clock—how much time had passed since you last were told the time!

CURRENT TIME PUZZLE

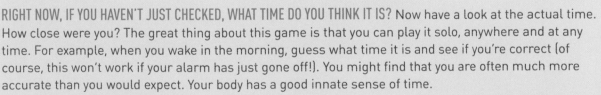

RIGHT NOW, IF YOU HAVEN'T JUST CHECKED, WHAT TIME DO YOU THINK IT IS? Now have a look at the actual time. How close were you? The great thing about this game is that you can play it solo, anywhere and at any time. For example, when you wake in the morning, guess what time it is and see if you're correct (of course, this won't work if your alarm has just gone off!). You might find that you are often much more accurate than you would expect. Your body has a good innate sense of time.

ORIENTATION PUZZLE

YOU'LL NEED A FRIEND AGAIN FOR THIS—preferably someone you can trust because you're going to be closing your eyes and relying on them! Stand in the center of a room and make a note of which way you're facing, and then close your eyes and have your friend gently turn you around and around on the spot for several seconds. (If at any point you start to feel dizzy, ask them to stop immediately so that you don't fall over!)

Now, without opening your eyes, try to point in the direction you were originally facing. Then open your eyes and see how close you were. How did you do?

BALANCE PUZZLE

THIS IS AN ACTIVITY YOU CAN TRY ALL ON YOUR OWN, ALTHOUGH IT MIGHT BE A LITTLE EASIER WITH A FRIEND. If you don't have a friend with you, find a place you can stand where you can quickly grab hold of something and lean on it if you need to. Next, set up a timer that you can see, or a countdown alarm that you can hear, so that you can measure the passage of 30 seconds of time.

Now, without holding on to anything, try balancing on one leg for 30 seconds. If you start to wobble, use your friend or the item next to you to lean against briefly, but then let go again as soon as you regain your balance. Can you make it to 30 seconds without any help at all?

Once you've balanced on one leg, try doing the same activity again on the other leg, too. (This might involve moving to face the other way, if you're standing next to an object for leaning on.)

Even if you find balancing like this difficult, if you practice often enough, you will usually start to get better, so it's not a bad thing to try!

NUMBER PYRAMID ANSWERS PAGE 145

COMPLETE THE NUMBER PYRAMID BY WRITING A NUMBER IN EACH EMPTY SQUARE. Every square in the pyramid must contain a value exactly equal to the total of the two squares immediately beneath it.

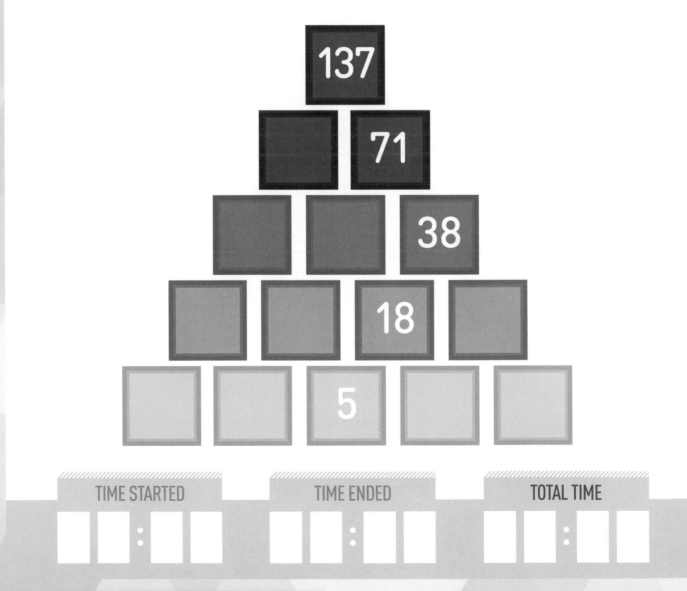

TIME STARTED

TIME ENDED

TOTAL TIME

A version of these puzzles will appear at the end of each chapter. After you solve them, record at the bottom of the page how long it took you to complete each puzzle. See if you can beat your own time as you work your way through chapter by chapter! You can use a timer or just consult a clock when you begin and when you finish.
→ **Are you ready to tackle some timed puzzles? Grab a pencil and get started!**

SIMPLE LOOP ANSWERS PAGE 145

DRAW A SINGLE CLOSED LOOP THAT VISITS EVERY WHITE SQUARE EXACTLY ONCE AND CROSSES NO BLUE SQUARES.
The loop can consist of only horizontal and vertical lines, and it cannot cross over or touch itself in any way.

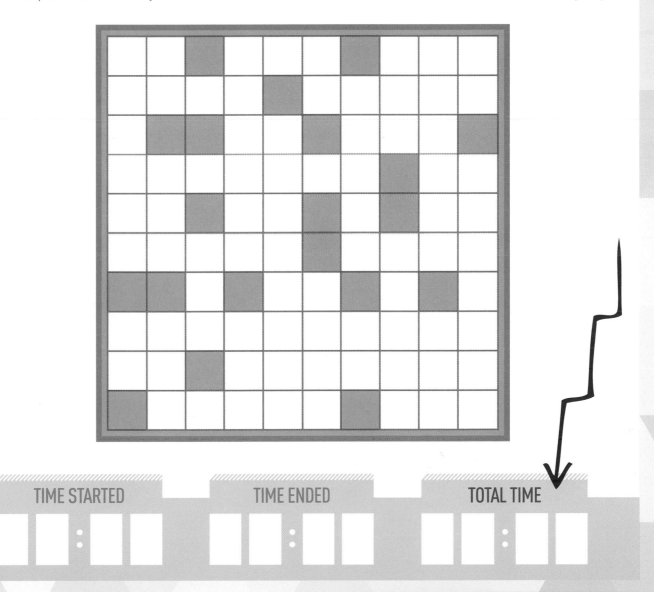

TIME STARTED

TIME ENDED

TOTAL TIME

CHAPTER THREE
WORDS AND LANGUAGE

Dolphins use squeaks and whistles to call each other by name. Parrots can repeat sounds they hear; some bored birds have even been known to mimic the sound of a doorbell or bark like a dog! But as far as we know, humans are the only creatures on Earth that use complex language to communicate. Turn the page to find out how your noggin works on words.

→

WORD **PATH**

ANSWERS PAGE 146

HOW MANY WORDS OF THREE OR MORE LETTERS CAN YOU FIND IN THIS GRID? Find words by starting on any square and then moving to horizontally, vertically, or diagonally touching squares. Keep moving to touching squares until you've spelled out your word. You can't visit any square more than once in a single word.

BONUS! There is one word that uses all 12 squares—can you find it?

R	S	A	R
E	H	D	I
S	S	E	R

ANSWERS →

→HEAR YE, HEAR YE!

WHEN SOMEONE ASKS YOU A QUESTION, THE SOUND PASSES INTO YOUR EARS AND THEN HEADS TO THE BRAIN'S AUDITORY AREA FOR PROCESSING.

Then, the signal travels to **Wernicke's area.** This part of the brain helps you interpret the information by recognizing patterns.

It's time to reply. **Broca's area,** which controls speech production, figures out what you should say in response.

Your brain's **motor area** sends signals to your vocal cords, tongue, and lips, which work together to speak your answer.

MYSTERIOUS MALADIES

People with speech problems have provided scientists with big clues about how the brain handles language.

In 1861, a French doctor named Paul Broca had a patient who could only say one word: "tan." Broca examined the man's brain and found that there was damage to a small part of his left frontal lobe. That part is now called **Broca's area.** People with damage to

Broca's area can understand language perfectly well, but they have trouble speaking.

In 1876, a German doctor named Carl Wernicke found that language problems could also be caused by damage to another part of the brain, now called **Wernicke's area.** People with damage to Wernicke's area can speak clearly, but they can't understand language. Their speech is made up of words all mixed together and doesn't make sense.

In 97 percent of people, both Broca's and Wernicke's areas are located on the left side of the brain. In 1960, researchers found a way to temporarily put parts of

WERNICKE'S AREA

BROCA'S AREA

the brain to sleep. When the right side of someone's brain was asleep, the person could speak and answer questions. But when the left side was asleep, the person could think but not talk.

YOUR BRAIN ON MUSIC

Though music has been part of every human culture for as long as we have been recording history—and though babies react to music before they can even talk!—there is no music center in the brain. Different people use different brain areas when they're listening to a beat.

Music can improve your mood. And, of course, practicing an instrument makes you better at playing music. But it might also boost your brain in other ways. In 2014, scientists found that after taking music lessons for two years, a group of kids didn't just get better at the drums or guitar—they also got better at processing language.

LANGUAGE DOESN'T JUST MEAN SPEECH. THE GESTURES USED BY DEAF PEOPLE IN SIGN LANGUAGE ARE ANALYZED BY THE BRAIN'S VISUAL AREA, BUT THEY ACTIVATE THE LANGUAGE AREAS OF THE BRAIN THE SAME WAY VERBAL SPEECH DOES.

THE FIRST MUSICAL INSTRUMENTS WERE CARVED BONES AND ANIMAL SKINS STRETCHED OVER HOLLOW TREE STUMPS SOME 40,000 YEARS AGO.

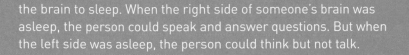

LETTER SOUP

ANSWERS PAGE 146

THE NAMES OF FIVE DIFFERENT COLORS ARE MUDDLED UP IN THE PICTURE AT RIGHT, and their letters have flown all over the place. Can you figure out what they are? When you finish, you'll have used each letter once. Hint: The color names are all at least five letters long.

ANSWERS →

BACK-TO-BACK ANSWERS PAGE 146

COMPLETE EACH OF THE FOLLOWING WORDS by adding the same letter to both the start and the end of the word. For example, you would add an S to _TAG_ to make STAGS.

HOUGH

TARE

ROM

EADE

OZE

UMM

_LS_

Here are the letters you will need: A, D, E, R, S, T, Y

MISSING LETTERS
ANSWERS PAGE 146

EACH OF THE FOLLOWING SENTENCES IS MISSING A SINGLE LETTER.
Find the single letter that can replace all the question marks on a line.

___   ?o?'s ?o? ?ade ?any yu??y su??erti?e ?eals.

___   Go?f ba??s ro?? we??.

___   ?a?a's a??ou?ci?g ru??ing eve?ts ?ow.

___   ?re?ory's ?i??lin? at sta??erin?ly ?ood ?a?s.

DELETED PAIRS ANSWERS PAGE 146

REMOVE ONE LETTER FROM EACH PAIR OF LETTERS in order to spell out a word.
For example, CD OE GU would become ~~C~~D ~~O~~E ~~G~~U to spell DOG.

CD AE TO   ANSWER →

LT IE PD EN   ANSWER →

WL OE NV EP ST   ANSWER →

SC LI NE SV EU RT   ANSWER →

PD RS EA AO NM OE RT ANSWER →

CRYPTOGRAM

ANSWERS PAGE 146

CAN YOU CRACK THIS CODE? Each letter has been replaced by the letter that comes immediately after it in the alphabet. So, in the sentences below, B has replaced A, C has replaced B, D has replaced C, and so on and so on throughout the entire alphabet.

Dpohsbuvmbujpot po efdpejoh uijt tfdsfu nfttbhf. Zpv bsf b nbtufs tpmwfs!

ANSWER →

BROKEN WORDS

ANSWERS PAGE 146

REARRANGE EACH OF THE FOLLOWING groups of word fragments to spell out an animal. For example, OP LE ARD would rearrange to LE OP ARD, spelling LEOPARD.

NK EY MO — ANSWER →

EE CH TAH — ANSWER →

RAF GI FE — ANSWER →

OC IN ER OS RH — ANSWER →

EE IM NZ CH PA — ANSWER →

RK AA VA RD — ANSWER →

ANAGRAM SETS

ANSWERS PAGE 146

CAN YOU FIND FOUR PAIRS OF ANAGRAMS in this set of twenty words? For example, you could pair TIME and MITE if they were included, since they are anagrams of one another. (Remember: An anagram is a word formed by rearranging the letters of another word.)

STIFLE	DIGEST	ITSELF	BULKED
SERIES	SINEWS	ORIENT	VASTER
BAMBOO	HIGHLY	GIGGLE	PERILS
LEAVES	AVERTS	SWINES	CAPPED
PLIERS	INVEST	UNDONE	CLOVER

ANSWER →

ANSWER →

ANSWER →

ANSWER →

ONCE YOU'VE COMPLETED THE ABOVE SET, can you find two pairs in this set?

STANZAS	BUNNIES	BROADEN	BUTTONS
ANALOGY	FROWNED	THICKEN	MANGLED
DESCENT	DOLLIES	MEANEST	KITCHEN
SKIDDED	SCENTED	FATEFUL	MATURED
HOARSER	MISTAKE	PAUPERS	BINDING

ANSWER →

ANSWER →

"STATELY" ANAGRAMS

ANSWERS PAGE 146

CAN YOU REARRANGE THE LETTERS in each of these amusing phrases to reveal the names of U.S. states? Ignore the spaces—they're just there to confuse you!

COOL ROAD
ANSWER →

SEEN TEENS
ANSWER →

A FRAIL COIN
ANSWER →

A REAL DEW
ANSWER →

SAW NOTHING
ANSWER →

IN NAVY PLANES
ANSWER →

WORD CHAINS
ANSWERS PAGE 146

BY CHANGING JUST ONE LETTER AT EACH STEP, and without rearranging any of the letters, can you convert each word at the top of these chains into the word at the bottom? The first one is done for you as an example.

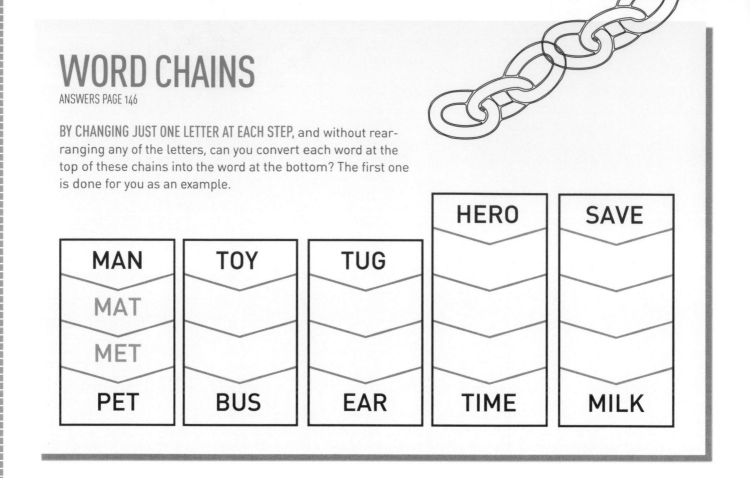

MAN	TOY	TUG	HERO	SAVE
MAT				
MET				
PET	BUS	EAR	TIME	MILK

WORD PYRAMID
ANSWERS PAGE 146

FIND THE MISSING WORD from each sentence to fill this word pyramid. Each of its six rows of letters contains all the letters from the row above plus one extra letter.

1. When you refer to one of something, you might say "I have ___cat."
2. ____ is a two-letter word that means "father."
3. You might use a ____ when you cook.
4. When you work out how to tackle something, you come up with a _____.
5. If you fly somewhere, you will probably do so on a _____.
6. Within the solar system, Earth is the third _____.

LINK WORDS

ANSWERS PAGE 146

FIND A WORD THAT CAN BE ADDED TO THE END of the first word and the beginning of the second word to form two new, different words. For example, if you had BIRTH _____ DREAM, you could add DAY to the middle to form BIRTHDAY and DAYDREAM.

FOR _____ TEN

BASE _____ GAME

DOWN _____ SIDE

CROSS _____ WAY

EAR _____ STICKS

PARTIAL TITLES

ANSWERS PAGE 146

SOME FAMOUS BOOKS that were made into movies have been written below, but only half of the letters have been given. For example, *How the Grinch Stole Christmas!* might be written as H_W _H_ G_I_C_ S_O_E _H_I_T_A_!

Can you fill in the blanks to reveal the titles?

H_R_Y _OT_R _N_ T_E _O_C_R_R'_ S_O_E

_H_R_I_ A_D _H_ C_O_O_A_E _A_T_R_

_O_ T_ T_A_N _OR _R_G_N

D_A_Y _F _ W_M_Y _I_

_H_ C_T _N _H_ H_T

CROSSWORD ANSWERS PAGE 146

SOLVE THE CLUES TO FILL IN THIS CROSSWORD GRID. Write the answers in horizontally for the across clues and vertically for the down clues. The number of letters in each word is in parentheses after the clue.

Across

1. Large seabird with a big pouch in its beak for holding fish (7)
5. A long, narrow piece of equipment you wear under a boot to glide over snow (3)
7. Past tense of "light," as in "I ____ the candle" (3)
8. Another word for snake (7)
9. A journey that stops at several places (4)
10. A soft, soothing shade of a color (Hint: Pink and baby blue are two examples.) (6)
13. Cheddar, Swiss, and mozzarella are examples (6)
14. Mythical, hairy snow monster (4)
16. A person who plays sports (7)
18. Honey-making insect (3)
19. Where the sun, moon, and stars are (3)
20. You work on a group ____ with your classmates. (7)

Down

1. Elected people who run the country (11)
2. Green, leafy salad vegetable (7)
3. People sometimes put their cell phone in a ____ to protect it. (4)
4. Ordinary, not unusual (6)
5. Look at something with your eyes (3)
6. Smart or brainy (11)
11. Shake with fear (7)

12. You are usually in bed with your eyes closed when you are this (6)
15. Person who does something brave (4)
17. Dry grass, used as food for animals (3)

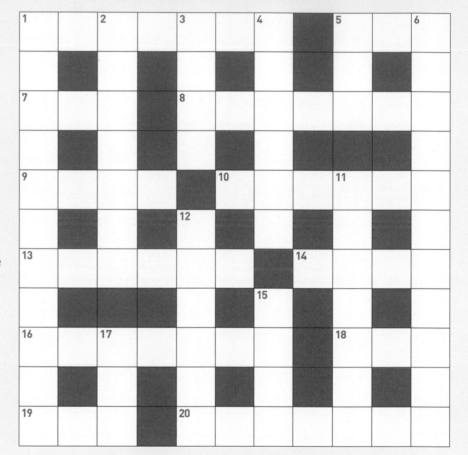

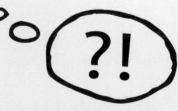

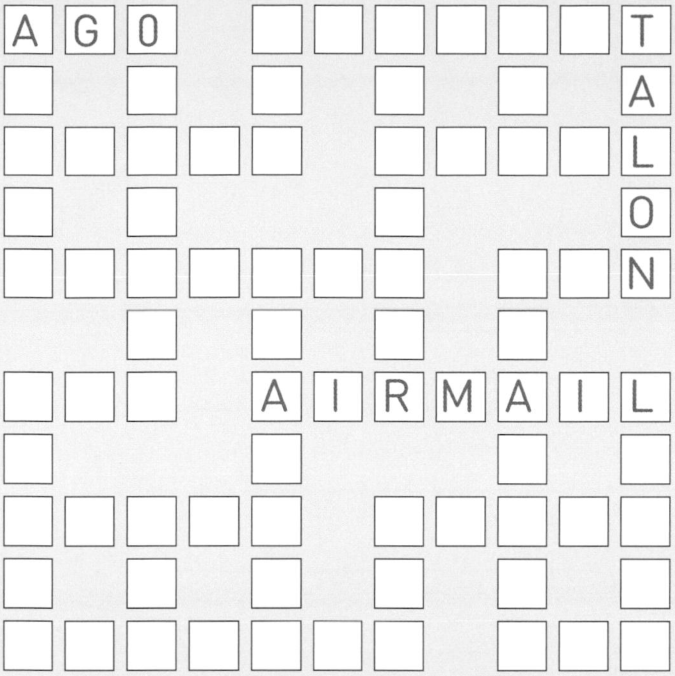

WORD FIT

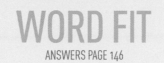

ANSWERS PAGE 146

CAN YOU FIT ALL THE LISTED WORDS INTO THE GRID? Place words horizontally or vertically, one letter per box. We've added in a few to get you started.

3 letters	5 letters	7 letters
~~Ago~~	Allow	~~Airmail~~
Art	Atlas	Emperor
Ash	Enter	Ostrich
Eat	Large	Pharaoh
Eel	Latin	Present
Pen	Llama	Satchel
Rye	Petal	Toaster
Tan	~~Talon~~	Whisper

WORD SEARCH

ANSWERS PAGE 146

FIND ALL THE LISTED PRESIDENTS IN THE GRID. They can be written in any direction, including diagonally, and can read either forward or backward.

BUCHANAN	HOOVER	MONROE
BUSH	JEFFERSON	OBAMA
COOLIDGE	JOHNSON	ROOSEVELT
EISENHOWER	KENNEDY	WASHINGTON
FORD	LINCOLN	
GARFIELD	MCKINLEY	

C	O	O	L	I	D	G	E	T	F	N
N	G	A	R	F	I	E	L	D	N	A
C	O	H	M	A	E	E	G	L	O	N
A	N	T	M	C	V	D	O	N	S	A
E	Y	A	G	E	K	C	R	N	R	H
M	B	D	S	N	N	I	O	O	E	C
O	M	O	E	I	I	S	N	W	F	U
N	O	I	L	N	N	H	S	L	F	B
R	E	W	O	H	N	E	S	I	E	O
O	S	H	O	O	V	E	R	A	J	Y
E	O	J	B	U	S	H	K	O	W	N

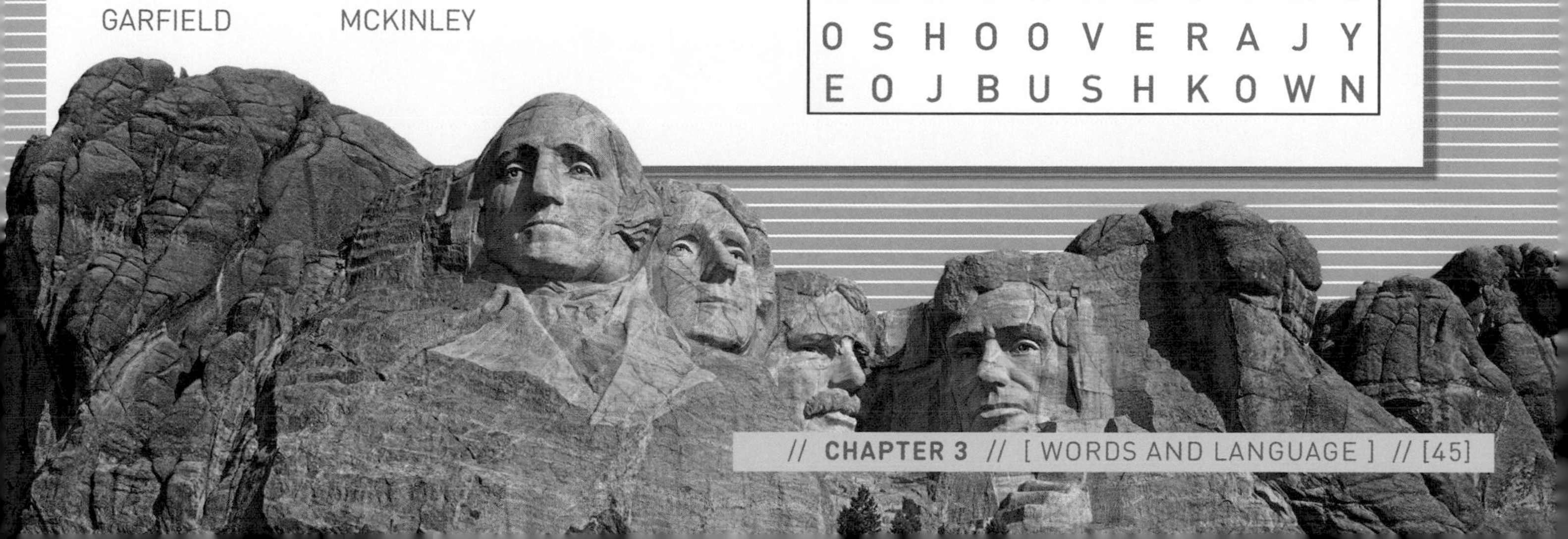

WORD ANALOGIES
ANSWERS PAGE 147

CAN YOU COMPLETE EACH OF THE FOLLOWING WORD-ANALOGY STATEMENTS?

Hexagon is to six, as square is to _____.

Wet is to dry, as dirty is to _____.

Bronze is to third, as gold is to _____.

Mouth is to face, as fingers are to _____.

Egg is to bird, as seed is to _____.

FIND THE SETS
ANSWERS PAGE 147

THE FOLLOWING 18 WORDS CAN BE ARRANGED INTO 6 SETS, each with 3 words in it. The words in each set all share a common connection, such as all being types of vegetables. Be careful, though, because some words can fit into multiple sets, but there is only one way of forming all 6 sets without using a word more than once.

EARTH	COPPER	GOLD
IRON	WASH	BANANA
ORANGE	SOIL	SATURN
BRONZE	VENUS	RED
MERCURY	YELLOW	MUD
GREEN	APPLE	DRY

ANSWER →

ANSWER →

ANSWER →

ANSWER →

ANSWER →

ANSWER →

ODD WORD OUT ANSWERS PAGE 147

WHICH IS THE ODD WORD OUT IN EACH OF THESE SETS OF FIVE WORDS?
Four of the words all have something in common that the fifth one doesn't.

OOPS!

Dog, Elephant, Lizard, Mouse, Skunk

ANSWER →

Red, Yellow, Violet, White, Indigo

ANSWER →

Six, One, Twelve, Twenty, Eight

ANSWER →

Myth, Gym, Rhythm, Worm, Hymn

ANSWER →

Spear, Prose, Spare, Parse, Pears

ANSWER →

OPPOSITES ATTRACT ANSWERS PAGE 147

DRAW LINES TO JOIN EACH WORD in the left-hand
column to its opposite in the right-hand column.
You will notice that some words can be the
opposite of more than one other word, but in
this puzzle there is only one solution where each
word is in a single pair and all words are used.

LOUD	WHITE
COME	HARD
EASY	DARK
SOFT	HATE
LIGHT	QUIET
BLACK	FAR
NEAR	DIFFICULT
LOVE	GO

VOWEL PLAY

ANSWERS PAGE 147

ALL THE VOWELS HAVE BEEN DELETED FROM THE
FOLLOWING WORDS. Can you restore the vowels
and discover the original words?

WNDRFL   ANSWER →

VRYDY   ANSWER →

TMRRW   ANSWER →

PLSNT   ANSWER →

WLDBST   ANSWER →

ZCCHN   ANSWER →

VOWEL TITLES

ANSWERS PAGE 147

THE VOWELS HAVE ALSO BEEN REMOVED FROM ALL
THE FOLLOWING MOVIE TITLES. Can you figure out
what the original titles were?

BTY ND TH BST   ANSWER →

TH WZRD F Z   ANSWER →

TY STRY   ANSWER →

TH NCRDBLS   ANSWER →

FRZN   ANSWER →

MRY PPPNS   ANSWER →

[BEHIND THE BRAIN]

Most people can read words that are missing letters with surprising ease. Even when the middle letters in a word are jumbled, or some
letters are replaced with digits, our brains don't have too much trouble deciphering the message. Scientists think our ability to read
garbled messages has to do with our brain's strength at recognizing patterns. Your brain thinks of words that include these letters, then
fills in the missing ones.

ANAGRAM SENTENCES ANSWERS PAGE 147

FOR EACH SENTENCE BELOW, rearrange the letters in the highlighted word
to find a new word that can be placed into the gap to complete the sentence.

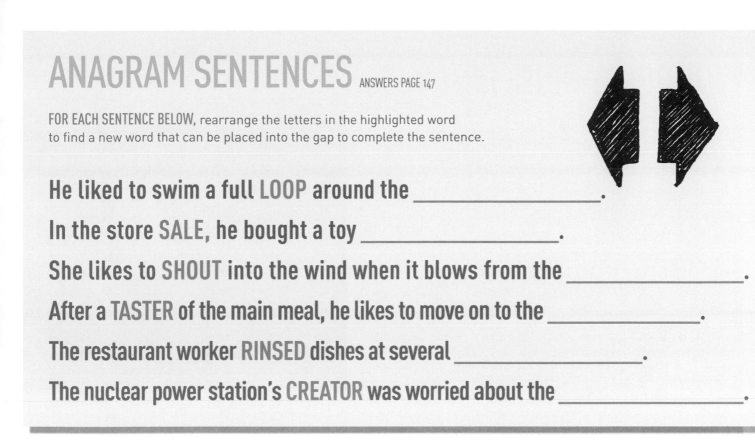

He liked to swim a full LOOP around the _____.

In the store SALE, he bought a toy _____.

She likes to SHOUT into the wind when it blows from the _____.

After a TASTER of the main meal, he likes to move on to the _____.

The restaurant worker RINSED dishes at several _____.

The nuclear power station's CREATOR was worried about the _____.

TWO-LETTER SEQUENCES

ANSWERS PAGE 147

CAN YOU WORK OUT WHICH LETTER SHOULD COME NEXT in each of these sequences?
They are all based on real-world sequences. For example, **Mo Tu We Th Fr Sa**
would be followed by **Su** since they are the days of the week: **Mo**nday, **Tu**esday,
Wednesday, **Th**ursday, **Fr**iday, and **Sa**turday, so **Su**nday comes next.

On Tw Th Fo Fi Si __
(Hint: Think about counting.)

Re Or Ye Gr Bl In __
(Hint: Think about colors.)

Ja Fe Ma Ap Ma Ju __
(Hint: Think about the calendar.)

Me Ve Ea Ma Ju Sa __
(Hint: Think about the solar system.)

Fi Se Th Fo Fi Si __
(Hint: Think about running a race.)

WORDPLAY RIDDLES ANSWERS PAGE 147

EACH OF THE FOLLOWING IS A RIDDLE based on wordplay. For example, if the question were "Which 11-letter phrase contains all 26 letters?," the answer could be "the alphabet."

1. What occurs once in a minute, twice in a moment, but not once in a thousand years?

   ANSWER →

2. What word is always spelled incorrectly?

   ANSWER →

3. What word becomes shorter when you add two letters to it?

   ANSWER →

4. What occurs once in January and once in February, but then doesn't occur again until June, July, and August?

   ANSWER →

5. What do you call a bear with a missing ear?

   ANSWER →

6. You know that one comes before two, but where does two come after three, and four before one?

   ANSWER →

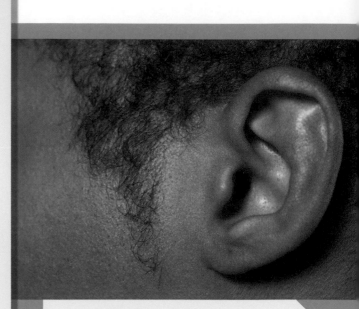

SOUNDALIKES

ANSWERS PAGE 147

TWO WORDS THAT SOUND THE SAME but are spelled differently are called homophones. Draw lines to join the pairs of homophones in this table of words:

FAZE	HOUR
REIGN	NIGHT
MAZE	WEATHER
EYE	I
SCENT	RAIN
KNIGHT	PHASE
WHETHER	MAIZE
OUR	CENT

HIDDEN PHRASES ANSWERS PAGE 147

EACH OF THESE FOUR BOXES CONTAINS A HIDDEN SHORT SAYING, such as "pass the buck."
By saying what you see, can you reveal each of the four sayings?

straw
straw
straw
→ straw

corners

BE the bush AT

ANSWER →

ANSWER →

ANSWER →

ANSWER →

LETTER CIRCLES ANSWERS PAGE 147

HERE'S A GREAT WORD GAME TO PLAY AGAINST OTHERS (but it's also fun to challenge yourself!). You'll need a timer of any sort—one from a board game, a timer on a phone, or a countdown timer on a watch will all work. Set the timer for three minutes.

When time starts, the aim is to find as many words as possible in a letter circle. There are six given below, but you can make up your own, too. A valid word must use three or more letters from the letter circle and must always include the center letter. You can't use a letter more times than it appears in the letter circle; if it only appears once, you can use it only once. Write down each word and, once time is up, add up your total to see who won. You might also need a dictionary to check any words you aren't sure about!

BONUS! Each of the letter circles on this page also has one word that uses every letter—can you find it?

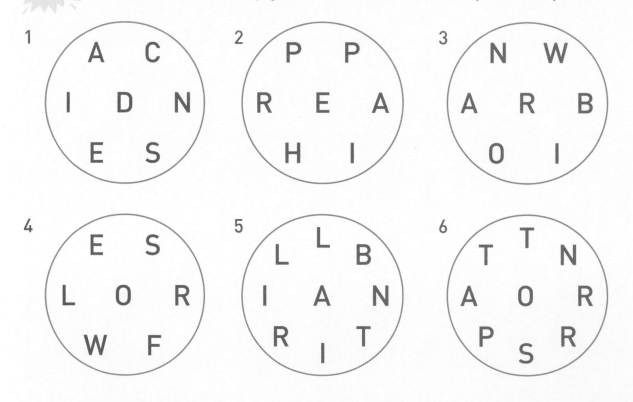

THE A TO Z GAME

HOW IS YOUR VOCABULARY? Do you think you could name a fruit or vegetable starting with every letter of the alphabet? Now's your chance to find out! Grab some friends and some paper and pens. You and your friends should each take a piece of paper and write each letter of the alphabet in a column down the left-hand side. Next, pick a topic; there are some suggestions below. Finally, decide on a time limit, such as five minutes, and then see if you can think of one word that starts with each letter of the alphabet, from A to Z, within that time limit. The word should be within your topic, so if you're looking for a vegetable starting with Z, then you are probably going to write "zucchini."

SUGGESTED TOPICS:

FRUITS AND VEGETABLES	COUNTRIES OF THE WORLD
TOWNS AND CITIES IN YOUR STATE	COLORS
MUSIC ARTISTS	MOVIE TITLES
BOOK TITLES	AUTHORS
TYPES OF CANDY	THINGS YOU FIND IN THE KITCHEN
TYPES OF CLOTHING	ACTORS AND ACTRESSES

WORD CONNECTIONS

THIS IS A GAME YOU CAN PLAY IN A GROUP OF ANY SIZE. You start with a single word, and then you take turns calling out a word that can immediately follow it to make a new word or expression by combining the two. So, for example, if the first word called out is "dog," the next person might say "house" to form "dog house." Then the person after them could say "boat," to form "house boat." Then the person after them could call out "race" to make "boat race" and so on.

Some suggested starting words are given below, but you can make up your own. Keep going clockwise around the group until someone cannot think of a word or expression; they are then eliminated. Start again with the person to their left with a new word and keep going until only one person is left. That last person is the winner! Tip: Avoid using plural words, because these are much harder to connect to.

SUGGESTED START WORDS:

SMART	BLACK	WHITE
NEXT	COMPUTER	MATH
REAL	TIME	MAJOR
PRIVATE	CENTER	FINAL

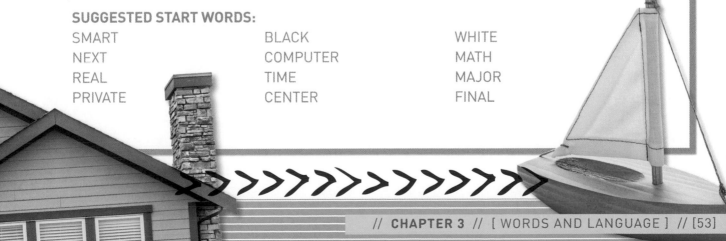

NUMBER PYRAMID ANSWERS PAGE 147

COMPLETE THE NUMBER PYRAMID BY WRITING A NUMBER IN EACH EMPTY SQUARE. Every square in the pyramid must contain a value exactly equal to the total of the two squares immediately beneath it.

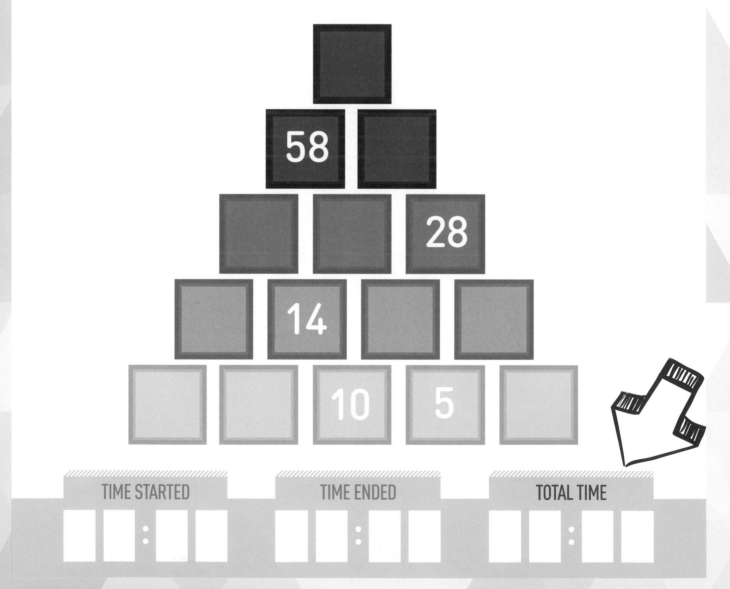

TIME STARTED

TIME ENDED

TOTAL TIME

SIMPLE LOOP ANSWERS PAGE 147

DRAW A SINGLE CLOSED LOOP THAT VISITS EVERY WHITE SQUARE EXACTLY ONCE AND CROSSES NO BLUE SQUARES.
The loop can consist of only horizontal and vertical lines and cannot cross over or touch itself in any way.

TIME STARTED

TIME ENDED

TOTAL TIME

CHAPTER FOUR

SPATIAL SMARTS

When you consider the types of intelligence there are, you probably think of math, writing, and maybe even art. But there's a key kind of braininess that often gets overlooked: spatial intelligence. This is the ability to think in three dimensions. It's essential for finding your way in a new city, solving a Rubik's Cube, or playing sports. You might not know it, but you use your spatial smarts every day!

→

IDEA

COIN **CONUNDRUM**

ANSWERS PAGE 148

FOR THIS CHALLENGE YOU'LL NEED FOUR COINS of the same value. Start by laying them out on the table like this:

Now, can you find a way to arrange them so that all four coins are touching every other coin?

MENTAL MAPMAKING

HOLDING YOUR TENNIS RACKET, YOU WATCH YOUR OPPONENT ACROSS THE NET AS SHE WINDS UP TO SERVE. *THWACK!* THE BALL COMES FLYING TOWARD YOU.

Neurons in your **parietal lobe** do some split-second math, calculating the speed and direction of the ball to create a mental map of its path across the court. Then these neurons calculate the path you should take to reach it. You take off toward the ball.

As you reach your target, other neurons adjust the position of your body. Your feet plant as your arms wind up.

Neurons in your **hippocampus** check your mental map to calculate which way to aim the ball. *Smack!* The ball sails off your racket into the corner of the court, out of your opponent's reach. You win the point!

SPATIAL SMARTS

Spatial intelligence is sometimes called visual thinking. Imagine that you're hiking in the woods with a compass and a map. There's no path for you to follow, but using the tools you have, you visualize a mental path to follow toward your destination.

Not all spatial thinking happens in 3-D. A chessboard is two-dimensional, but to win, you have to visualize the moves you and your opponent will make. The better you can keep track of pieces as you move them around in your mind, the better your chances are of becoming a chess champion.

Many standard intelligence tests don't measure spatial intelligence very well. That means people who are especially good at this type of thinking

HIPPOCAMPUS

PARIETAL LOBE

sometimes go unnoticed. But many skilled spatial thinkers go on to have successful careers in fields like engineering, physics, and computer science.

BRAIN BUILDING

In the classic puzzle game *Tetris*, color blocks fall from the sky while players flip and turn them to line them up. Released in the 1980s, it's now considered a classic: *Tetris* is the most popular computer game of all time. But it's not just fun to play. It may also help bulk up your brain.

In 2009, a team of scientists from New Mexico studied a group of teen girls as they played *Tetris* over a three-month period. Then, the team used MRI to take a peek at the girls' brains. They found that compared with girls who didn't play the game, parts of the players' frontal lobe got thicker. The study showed that using your brain for an activity like playing *Tetris* can actually change its shape.

PEOPLE WHO **SPEND HOURS** PLAYING *TETRIS* SOMETIMES REPORT THAT THEY **SEE FALLING BLOCKS IN THEIR DREAMS,** OR FIND THEMSELVES THINKING ABOUT HOW EVERYDAY OBJECTS COULD **FIT TOGETHER.** THIS EFFECT CAN HAPPEN WITH OTHER VIDEO GAMES, OR EVEN JIGSAW PUZZLES AND RUBIK'S CUBES. SCIENTISTS CALL IT **THE *TETRIS* EFFECT.**

CUBE NETS

ANSWERS PAGE 148

IMAGINE CUTTING OUT EACH OF THESE SHAPE "NETS" and then folding along the gray lines. Most of them would fold up to make perfect six-sided cubes, but there are three that would not. Can you figure out which three?

ODD CUBE OUT

ANSWERS PAGE 148

NOW IMAGINE CUTTING OUT AND FOLDING UP EACH OF THESE FOUR SHAPES. Three of them form identical six-sided cubes, but one does not. Which one?

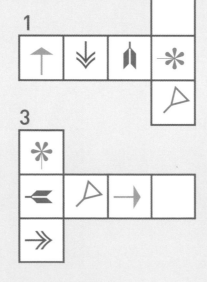
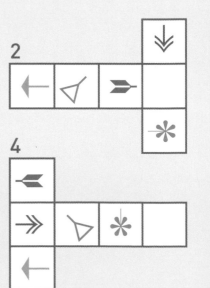

PYRAMID NETS ANSWERS PAGE 148

TWO OF THE SHAPE NETS BELOW CAN BE CUT OUT and folded to form a perfect four-sided triangle-based pyramid, and three can't. Which are the three?

A TRIANGLE-BASED
PYRAMID LOOKS LIKE THIS →

ODD PYRAMID OUT
ANSWERS PAGE 148

IMAGINE CUTTING OUT AND FOLDING UP THIS SHAPE to form a triangle-based pyramid. By rotating it around you would be able to see two of the images, A to C, but one of them would not be visible. Which is the odd one out?

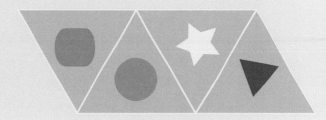

A
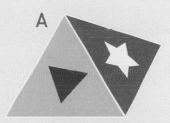

B

C
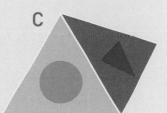

SHAPE LINK ANSWERS PAGE 148

THERE ARE TWO EACH OF SEVEN DIFFERENT SHAPES in both of the two grids below. Can you find a way to draw seven separate paths through the grid squares to connect each pair of identical shapes? Paths can travel only horizontally or vertically, and no more than one path can enter any square. This means that **paths cannot cross or touch at any point.**

PUZZLE 1

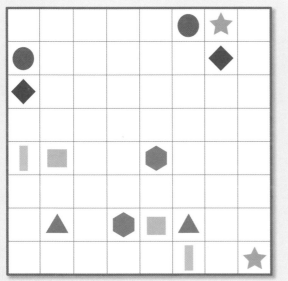

PUZZLE 2

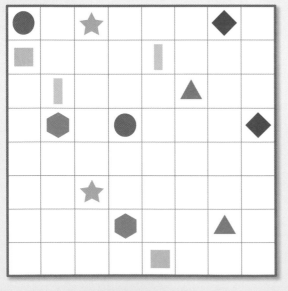

SHAPE DIVISION

ANSWERS PAGE 148

USING FOUR DIFFERENT COLORED PENCILS, shade in the boxes in the shapes below to divide up each of the two pictures into four separate shapes. Each of the shapes within a picture should be identical, although some of them may be rotated.

Here's an example:

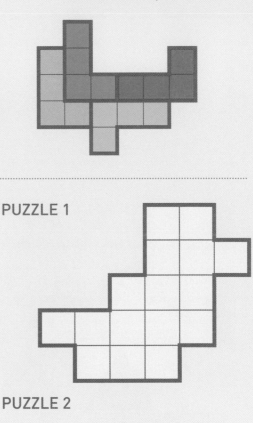

PUZZLE 1

PUZZLE 2

AREA DIVISION ANSWERS PAGE 148

CAN YOU DRAW JUST THREE STRAIGHT LINES in each of these pictures so that you end up with four separate areas? Each area should contain one of each different shape within the picture.

Here's one for you to help get you started:

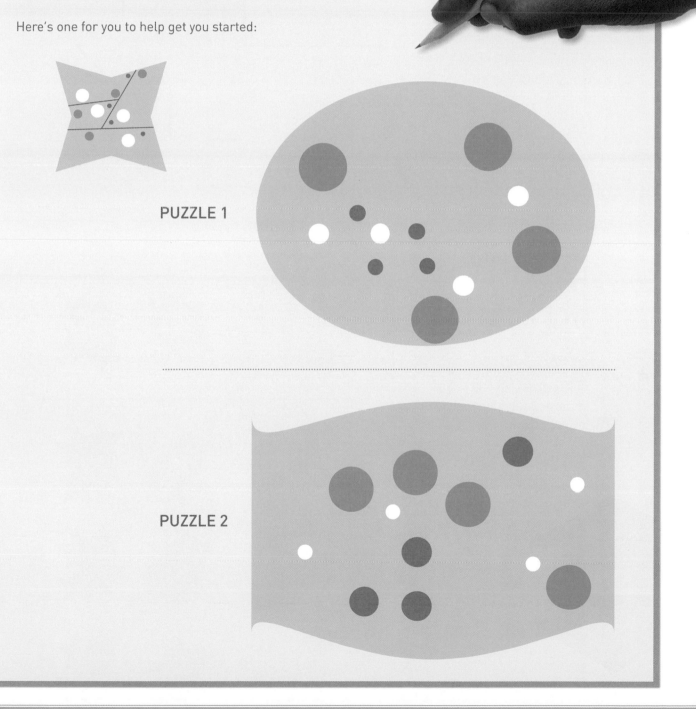

PUZZLE 1

PUZZLE 2

DRAW REFLECTIONS

ANSWERS PAGE 148

PRETEND THE BLUE VERTICAL DASHED LINE IS A MIRROR. Draw in each black line's "reflection" on the opposite side of it. You'll end up with a simple picture that looks a little like a robot's face!

IDENTITY REFLECTED

ANSWERS PAGE 148

FOR EACH OF THE THREE SIMPLE PICTURES ACROSS THE TOP of this image, identify which of the options, A to C, is the correct reflection of the picture in the pink mirror line.

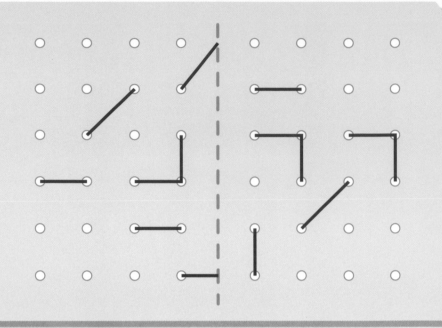

IDENTITY ROTATED

ANSWERS PAGE 148

FOR EACH OF THE THREE SIMPLE PICTURES ACROSS THE TOP of this image, identify which of the options, A to C, is the result of rotating the picture as shown by the arrow immediately underneath it—that is (from left to right), by 90 degrees clockwise, 180 degrees, or 90 degrees counterclockwise.

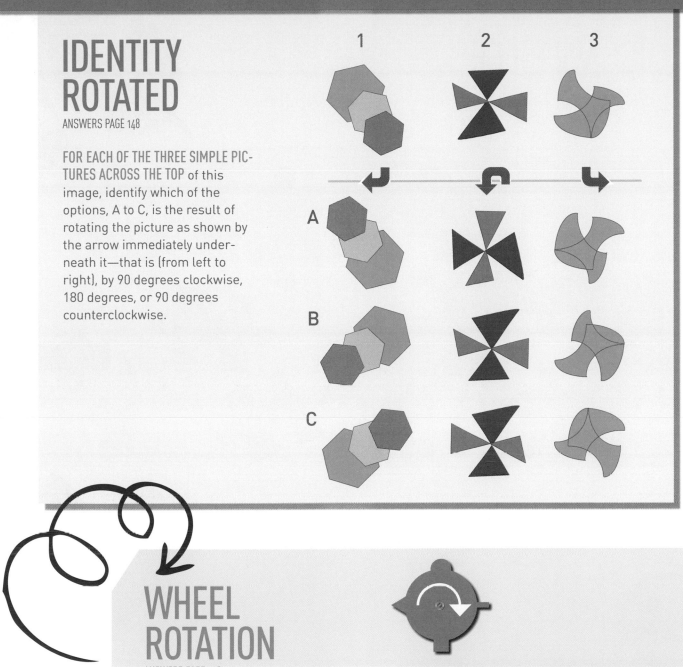

WHEEL ROTATION

ANSWERS PAGE 148

IMAGINE THAT YOU HAVE THE ORANGE WHEEL and are rolling it along the ground clockwise, as shown by the arrow. Which of the three rows of imprints could it leave in the ground?

JIGSAW PIECES ANSWERS PAGE 148

CAN YOU WORK OUT which of the various pieces can be used to finish the partially completed jigsaw?

KEY IMPRESSIONS

ANSWERS PAGE 148

WHICH OF THE IMPRESSIONS, A to C, would this key make if pushed down into soft modeling clay?

A   B   C

IMPOSSIBLE SHAPES

EACH OF THE FOLLOWING ARRANGEMENTS OF CUBES LOOKS PERFECTLY REASONABLE AT FIRST GLANCE, BUT WHEN YOU LOOK A BIT CLOSER, THERE'S SOMETHING NOT QUITE RIGHT!

Take a look at this arrangement of red cubes. Can you spot anything wrong with it? If you had a pile of cubes, could you actually build this structure?

The problem with this arrangement is that it can only be drawn, not built. If you were to try to build it, you might start off with the five cubes at the bottom; but if you then built up from each end, you'd soon discover that in reality the two sides wouldn't meet up at the top. The bottom-left cube would have to be two cubes closer than the cube at the bottom-right, but the bottom row is drawn as if the cubes are in a straight row. So this is an impossible shape.

HERE'S A FAMOUS IMPOSSIBLE SHAPE, DRAWN WITH CUBES. CAN YOU WORK OUT WHY THIS ARRANGEMENT WOULD BE IMPOSSIBLE TO MAKE, TOO?

Place your finger on the top-left cube, and then trace a line to the rightmost cube. If this was an actual physical object, you'd be coming forward toward yourself. Now trace a line from the rightmost cube to the bottom-left cube. This also comes forward toward you. So far so good! But now try tracing from the bottom-left cube up to the top-left cube. This goes straight up—but that doesn't make sense, because you know that in reality that cube would need to be farther away from you. So this arrangement of cubes is impossible to make.

OH!

3-D CUBE COUNTING ANSWERS PAGE 148

IMAGINE THAT YOU HAVE A 4×3×3 ARRANGEMENT OF CUBES, LIKE THIS:

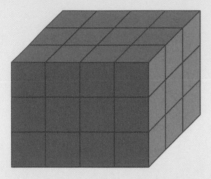

If some of them are removed, and the resulting arrange-ments look like this, how many cubes are left in each? Cubes can't be "floating" in midair, so if you can see a cube that isn't on the bottom level you can be sure the cubes underneath it are there, too.

$$1 + 2 = 3$$

SHAPE COUNTING

ANSWERS PAGE 148

HOW MANY RECTANGLES AND SQUARES of all sizes can you count in this picture? There are more than you might think ... including the one very large rectangle that runs all around the border of the picture!

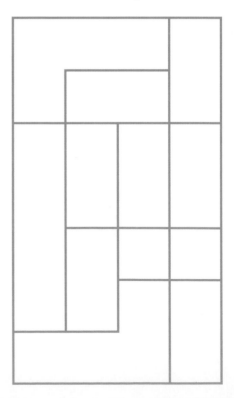

SLIDING LETTERS
ANSWERS PAGE 148

IMAGINE THE FOUR TILES SHOWN here are physical pieces that you can move around. By arranging them correctly, you can form a letter of the alphabet. Can you figure out which one?

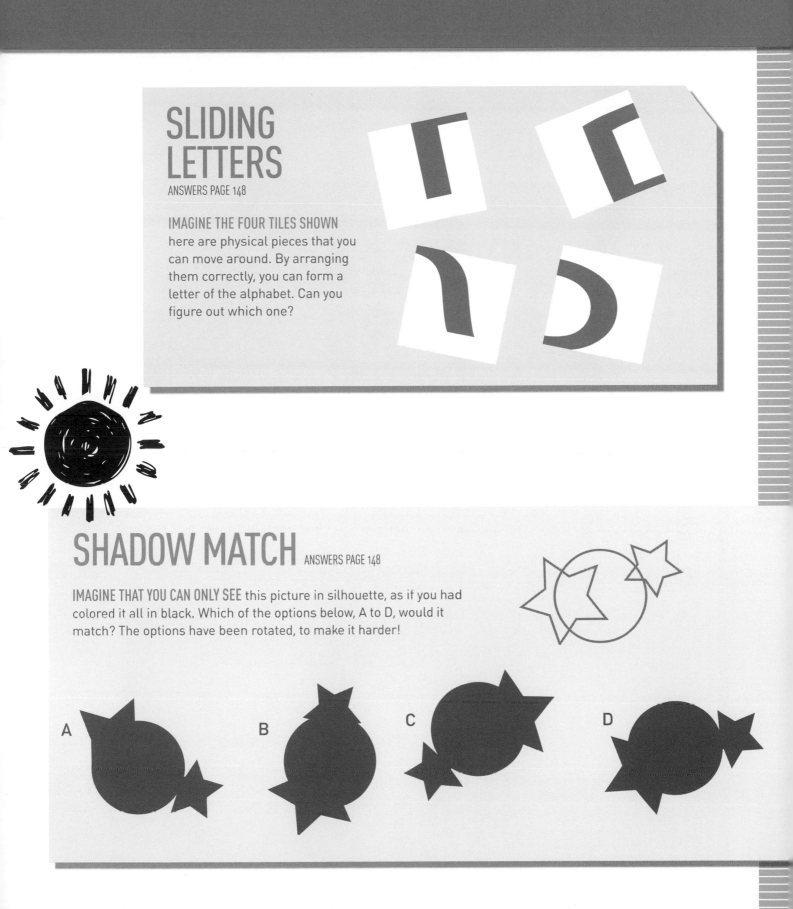

SHADOW MATCH ANSWERS PAGE 148

IMAGINE THAT YOU CAN ONLY SEE this picture in silhouette, as if you had colored it all in black. Which of the options below, A to D, would it match? The options have been rotated, to make it harder!

A

B

C

D

MAP ROTATION ANSWERS PAGE 148

YOU'RE IN A CITY YOU'RE NOT FAMILIAR WITH and you have the map shown at right. You're at the location marked "Here" at the bottom right, and you want to get to the airport, marked over on the far left of the map with the gray airplane symbol. You're facing in the direction shown by the red arrow.

Which one of the following sequences of instructions will get you to the airport?

1. Cross the river and take the second right. Turn left at the intersection, and then turn right as soon as you can. Cross over the next two intersections and then turn left. Follow the road around the corner, and then turn right. The airport is on your left.

2. Cross the river and then continue through the next four intersections. Turn right at the following intersection and then turn left. The airport is on your left.

3. Cross the river and turn left at the third intersection. Turn right at the first opportunity; then turn left at the end of the road. Turn right at the next intersection and then turn right at the first opportunity after that. The airport is on your left.

[BEHIND THE BRAIN]

For some people, reading a map is easy. For others, it's a surefire way to get lost. Map reading requires a certain set of spatial reasoning skills. The most important one is the ability to relate where you are in the real world to the same spot on a map. Another is the ability to mentally rotate the map as you go along your route.

MAP READING

ANSWERS PAGE 148

CAN YOU NOW WRITE OUT YOUR OWN INSTRUC-TIONS for the shortest route to the hospital, marked with an "H"? Use the same map and start again at the marker at the bottom-right, facing as shown by the red arrow.

When writing your instructions, it's best to keep them simple by describing each route in terms of the intersections. Then, once you're on the correct road, finish by describing where the destination is—for example, on the left.

ROUTE TO THE HOSPITAL:
ANSWER →

Then, once you've written a route to the hospital, can you also write down the short-est route to the gas station, marked with the gas pump symbol?

ROUTE TO THE GAS STATION:
ANSWER →

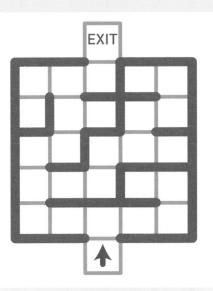

MAZE SOLVING

ANSWERS PAGE 149

WHICH ONE OF THESE SETS OF INSTRUCTIONS will successfully navigate you through this maze? Imagine that you are standing in the square with the red arrow, and you are facing into the maze in the direction shown by that arrow. You then walk step-by-step through each square of the grid, following the instructions.
The instructions consist of three different symbols, which mean:

⇧ **Move one square in the direction you are facing**

⇦ **Stay in the same square, but turn to face 90 degrees to your left**

⇨ **Stay in the same square, but turn to face 90 degrees to your right**

Remember that the instructions are all relative to the direction you are facing.

1 ⇧⇨⇧⇧⇧⇨⇧⇦⇧⇧⇨⇧⇧⇧⇦⇧

2 ⇧⇦⇧⇧⇨⇧⇧⇨⇧⇦⇧⇧⇨⇧⇦⇧

3 ⇧⇦⇧⇧⇨⇧⇧⇧⇦⇧⇨⇧⇦⇧⇨⇧

JOIN THE DOTS

ANSWERS PAGE 149

CAN YOU DRAW A SINGLE PATH made up from just four straight lines to connect all nine of these dots? It's trickier than you might expect!

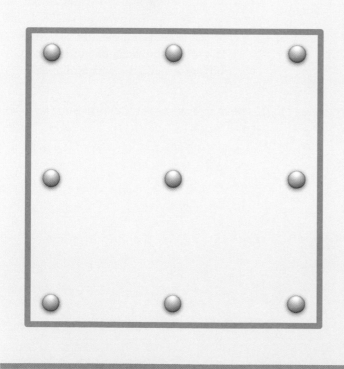

BOX THE DOTS

ANSWERS PAGE 149

CAN YOU ADD TWO SQUARES to this arrangement of nine dots so that you end up with nine separate areas and exactly one dot per area? The squares don't touch the dots.

DOT TO DOT ANSWERS PAGE 149

HERE'S A CONNECT-THE-DOTS PUZZLE WITH TWO TWISTS!

You should join the dots in increasing numerical order, just like in a regular connect the dots, except that
- you must do it in your imagination, without drawing on the paper, and
- you should only join numbers that are multiples of 3. So start with the 3, join to the 6, and so on.

What shape do you end up with?

PLUGS AND SOCKETS ANSWERS PAGE 149

WHICH OF THESE PAIRS of building blocks will fit together? The blue bricks snap on top of the orange bricks, with the dark connecting studs lining up with the white holes on the blue bricks. There is just one twist: You are looking at the under-side of the blue bricks, so you will need to imagine what they look like when turned over to fit on top of the orange bricks. Draw lines to join each connecting pair.

3-D VIEWS ANSWERS PAGE 149

IF YOU WERE TO VIEW this arrangement of cubes from directly above, looking down, what would you see? Shade in the view of the cubes that you would see from above in the upper grid. Then do the same with the grid to the right for what you would see when looking at the cube arrangement from the right.

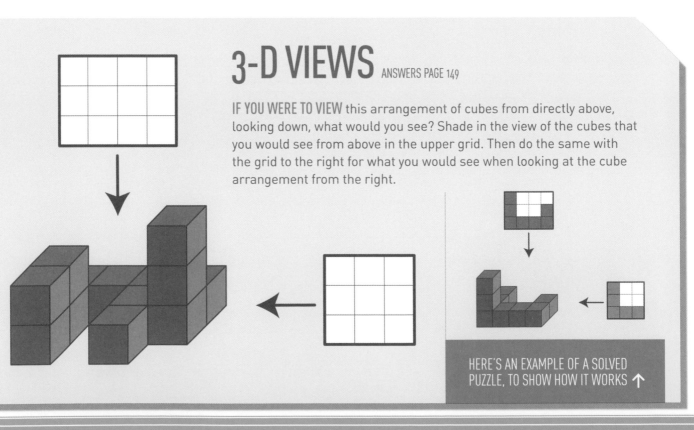

HERE'S AN EXAMPLE OF A SOLVED PUZZLE, TO SHOW HOW IT WORKS ↑

3-D ROTATIONS ANSWERS PAGE 149

WHICH ONE OF THE IMAGES, A to F, is a rotated version of the same arrangement of cubes shown in green? Try considering each level of the arrangement separately, rather than looking at the entire arrangement all at once. You could also try counting the number of cubes on a level; if this differs, you don't need to worry about their exact positions once rotated because you already know they don't match!

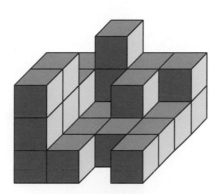

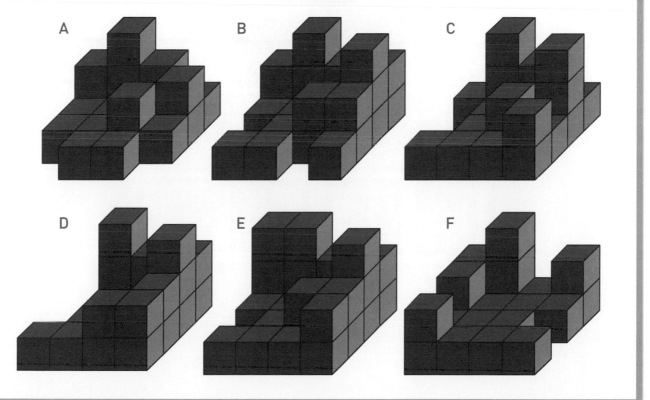

A

B

C

D

E

F

NUMBER PYRAMID ANSWERS PAGE 149

COMPLETE THE NUMBER PYRAMID BY WRITING A NUMBER IN EACH EMPTY SQUARE. Every square in the pyramid must contain a value exactly equal to the total of the two squares immediately beneath it.

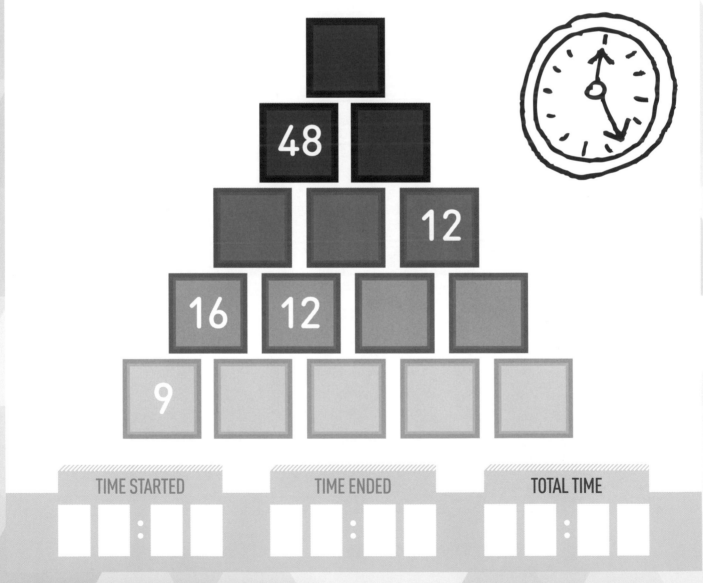

TIME STARTED

TIME ENDED

TOTAL TIME

SIMPLE LOOP ANSWERS PAGE 149

DRAW A SINGLE CLOSED LOOP THAT VISITS EVERY WHITE SQUARE EXACTLY ONCE AND CROSSES NO BLUE SQUARES.
The loop can consist of only horizontal and vertical lines and cannot cross over or touch itself in any way.

TIME STARTED

TIME ENDED

TOTAL TIME

CHAPTER FIVE

PROBLEM SOLVING

Aha! Everyone knows the feeling you get when the answer to a problem you've been puzzling over finally comes to you. Often, it happens when you're least expecting it. So what's going on in your brain when it's figuring out a problem?

Problem solving happens in your frontal lobe, the part of your brain that lies behind your forehead. This part of your brain controls complex thought, like thinking, planning, and organizing, as well as many aspects of your personality and emotions.

→

LIQUID **PROBLEM**

ANSWERS PAGE 150

YOU HAVE THREE JARS, with volumes of 2 pints, 5 pints, and 7 pints. The 2- and 5-pint jars are empty, but the 7-pint jar is full of water. Using just these jars, and no measuring equipment or other containers, how can you measure out exactly 6 pints of water?

ANSWER →

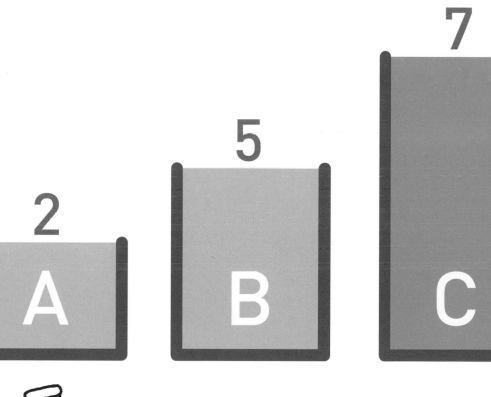

LOGICAL LEARNING

$$\{4y^2 - 1 + 2y\}^2 = 0$$

HAVE YOU EVER HEARD SOMEONE SAY THAT MATH IS THE UNIVERSAL LANGUAGE? IT'S TRUE! MOST CULTURES WORLDWIDE HAVE DEVISED NUMBER SYSTEMS AND WAYS OF REASONING WITH THEM.

We solve mathematical calculations by applying rules to numbers to arrive at an answer.

We can use the logical rules of numbers to communicate with people all around the world, even when we don't speak the same language.

INSIGHT

Another type of problem solving is called insight. That's the aha moment when a solution seems to appear out of nowhere. Have you ever gotten frustrated after trying and failing to master a song on the piano or understand a math equation and given up ... only to have the solution suddenly "click" in your brain? Then you've experienced insight problem solving.

You may not have been thinking about the problem before you arrived at the answer, but that doesn't mean your brain was being lazy. In 2009, a group of scientists placed volunteers in a functional MRI scanner to measure their brain activity. The researchers found that while people were daydreaming, the parts of their brains associated with solving problems weren't asleep at all—in fact, they were highly active! That suggests that our brains are always working on our problems, even when we don't know it. So the next time you catch yourself staring into space instead of doing your homework, don't beat yourself up—you're working on it!

ROBOT TAKEOVER?

Will robots rule the world someday? Since 2003, robotic vehicles called rovers have been exploring the dusty surface of Mars, where humans have yet to go. In 2011, in a fierce head-to-processor battle, a computer named Watson beat genius Ken Jennings on the quiz show *Jeopardy!* These achievements might suggest that robots have even become superior to the humans who make them.

But no computer ever built can match the power of the human brain. The Mars rovers can navigate around rocks and through sand by themselves—but they need humans to tell them their destination and what to do when they get there. Watson may have won a contest that has stumped some of the smartest humans—but its computer brain could only answer questions by searching a database of information. These robots lack the problem-solving skills that make humans so smart.

Here's what computer technology can't do (yet): solve problems that don't have a set of clear rules (like a doctor diagnosing a disease) or process brand new information (like a scientist discovering a medicine). All these skills involve thinking and reasoning as you go, something that is easy for humans to do but really hard for robots.

So, for now at least, the idea of robots taking over and ruling the world is just science fiction—thanks to your amazing brain.

MOST ARTIFICIAL INTELLIGENCE VOICES ARE FEMALE.

$$[4y^2 - 1]^2 + 2 \cdot 2y [4y^2 - 1] + (4y)^2 = 0$$

IT'S LOGICAL ANSWERS PAGE 150

THREE BROTHERS EACH HAVE DIFFERENT AGES AND HOBBIES. Can you figure out the age and hobby of each brother by using just the following clues? You can use the check-off chart to keep track of any deductions you make, if you wish.

- The youngest brother isn't Bart.
- The brother who likes singing is older than the brother who likes reading.
- Andy is older than Cliff.
- Bart isn't a fan of reading.
- The brother who likes singing is not Andy.
- The swimmer is older than the singer.

Brother	Age	Hobby

	Age			Hobby		
Brother	9 years	11 years	13 years	Swimming	Reading	Singing
Andy						
Bart						
Cliff						
Hobby Swimming						
Reading						
Singing						

SAND TIME CHALLENGE ANSWERS PAGE 150

IMAGINE THAT YOU HAVE TWO SAND TIMERS, one of which takes four minutes for the sand to flow through and the other of which takes five minutes for the sand to flow through. Using just these two timers, how can you measure exactly six minutes of time?

4:00   5:00

BALANCE ANSWERS PAGE 150

BY EXAMINING THE FOLLOWING PAIR OF BALANCES, can you work out which shape is the heaviest, and which shape is the lightest? (For the purposes of this puzzle, ignore the distance of a shape from the fulcrum.)

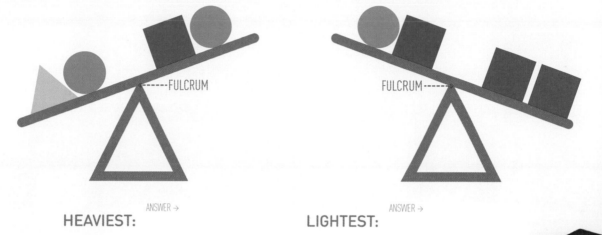

FULCRUM

FULCRUM

ANSWER →

ANSWER →

HEAVIEST:

LIGHTEST:

TOWER OF HANOI ANSWERS PAGE 150

TO PLAY THIS GAME YOU'LL NEED THREE OBJECTS of differing size to stack on top of one another, such as three books or perhaps three coins. You'll also need to choose three areas to place them. Mark one area as "A," the next as "B," and the final one as "C."

Start by putting all the objects in a pile at area "A," with the largest at the bottom and the smallest at the top. The aim of the game is to move all the objects to area "C" so they end up in the same order, with the largest on the bottom and the smallest on top.

Some rules:
1) You can move only the top object of a pile to another area.
2) You can place an object only on either a bigger object or directly on the ground.
3) You can never place a bigger object on top of a smaller object.

You might have seen versions of this game with disks and wooden pegs. They look like this:

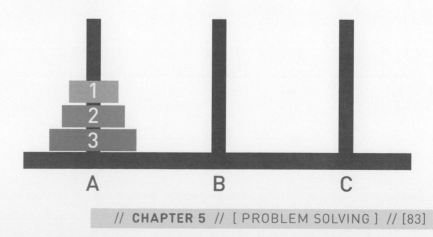

VISUAL SEQUENCES ANSWERS PAGE 150

CAN YOU FIGURE OUT which of the options comes next in each of these visual sequences?

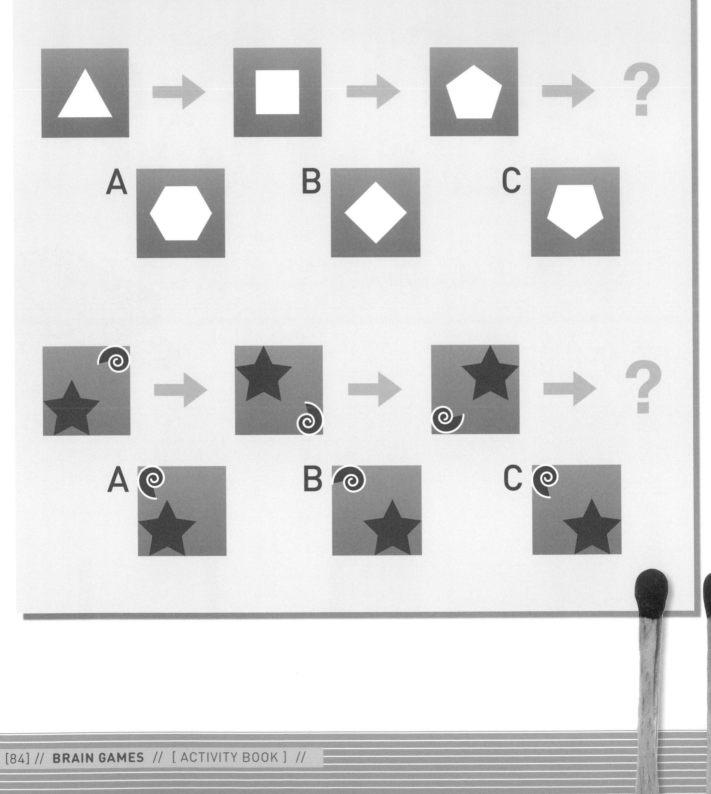

TIME CLASH
ANSWERS PAGE 150

THE NUMBERS 0 TO 9, WHEN DISPLAYED ON A DIGITAL CLOCK, LOOK LIKE THIS:

0123456789

If two numbers are overlapped, the result shows all the lit segments together, so for example if 1 and 2 are overlapped it looks like this:

Or if 3 and 7 are overlapped, it still looks like a 3 because the 7 doesn't add any new segments:

Each of the two clocks at right shows two times, but the two times have been overlapped. This means there are four times overall; all are different and are as follows:

5:10   7:22   8:30   10:34

Using your deductive skills, can you work out which two of the four times are overlapped on each of the clocks?

18:38

ANSWER →

19:88

ANSWER →

MATCHSTICKS
ANSWERS PAGE 150

CAN YOU FIGURE OUT HOW to turn these four squares into two squares by removing only two matches? All of the matches must be used by one of the two resulting squares, and you can't move any of the other matches.

NUMBER SEQUENCES ANSWERS PAGE 150

WHAT NUMBER COMES NEXT IN EACH OF THESE MATHEMATICAL SEQUENCES?

A) 6 9 12 15 18 _____

B) 29 25 21 17 13 _____

C) 2 4 8 16 32 _____

D) 243 81 27 9 3 _____

E) 13 17 19 23 29 _____

NUMBER DARTS

ANSWERS PAGE 150

BY PICKING ONE NUMBER from each ring of this dartboard, can you form each of the following totals? For example, to reach a total of 18 you would pick the number 3 from the inner (yellow) ring, the number 7 from the middle (orange) ring, and the number 8 from the outer (red) ring.

TOTALS:

19 ANSWER →

26 ANSWER →

33 ANSWER →

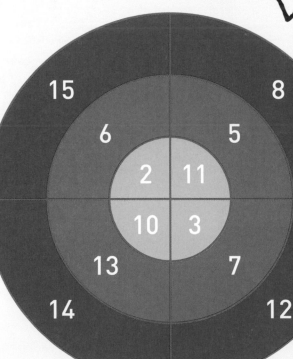

NUMBER ANAGRAMS ANSWERS PAGE 150

REARRANGE THE FOLLOWING NUMBERS AND MATH SIGNS to form each of the given results. You should use parentheses to create orders of operation. For example, you could form **43** with **(3 + 4) × 6 + 1 = 43**

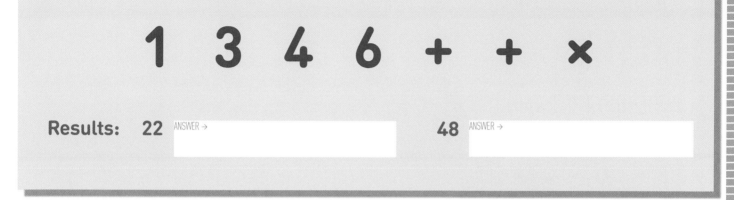

Results: **22** ANSWER →   **48** ANSWER →

NUMBER BUDDIES ANSWERS PAGE 150

CAN YOU FIND PAIRS OF NUMBERS that obey these mathematical rules of multiplication and division? So if, for example, the rule were **×3**, this means one of the numbers in each pair must be equal to the other number multiplied by three. Hint: You will use all the numbers, but each number can be used in only one pair.

RULE: ×2   12   6   40   34   5   10   20   3   24   17

ANSWER →

RULE: ×5   25   10   3   4   50   2   20   5   250   15

ANSWER →

RULE: ÷3   6   9   27   4   54   12   2   18   81   3

ANSWER →

SORTING SUMS ANSWERS PAGE 150

SEE HOW QUICKLY YOU CAN SORT each of these math calculations into increasing order of their result. Remember that you don't need to know the exact value of each result to sort them.

A: 35 × 3   **B: 3 × 17**   **C: 119 − 4**   **D: 193 × 174**   **E: 122 × 151**

ANSWER →

[BEHIND THE BRAIN]

In 2016, scientists used MRI (magnetic resonance imaging) to peek inside people's brains as they solved math problems. They discovered that the brain tackles number challenges in four steps: First you encode, or read and understand the problem. Then you plan, or figure out how to tackle it. Next you solve, or actually do the math. Last, you respond, or write down the answer.

NUMBER MAZE ANSWERS PAGE 150

CAN YOU FIND A ROUTE THROUGH THIS NUMBER MAZE? You can move to a circle only if its value is equal to the previous circle's value plus three or minus four. Enter at the given circle and follow lines to connected circles.

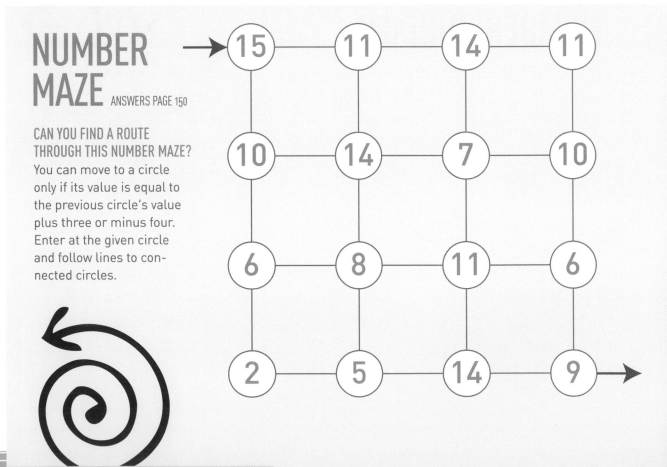

BRAIN CHAINS ANSWERS PAGE 151

START WITH THE VALUE ON THE LEFT of each of these brain chains, and then apply each math instruction in turn until you reach the "Result" box on the right. What value do you get in each case? Do the math in your head, rather than with pencil and paper or a calculator.

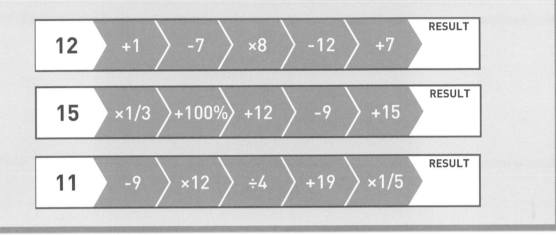

| 12 | +1 | -7 | ×8 | -12 | +7 | RESULT |

| 15 | ×1/3 | +100% | +12 | -9 | +15 | RESULT |

| 11 | -9 | ×12 | ÷4 | +19 | ×1/5 | RESULT |

RECTANGULAR DIVISION ANSWERS PAGE 151

DRAW BOLD LINES ALONG THE GRID LINES to divide the grid into a set of rectangles and squares. Each block must contain the number of grid squares indicated by the number inside it.

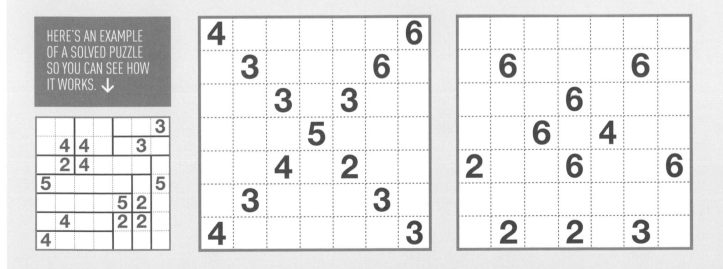

HERE'S AN EXAMPLE OF A SOLVED PUZZLE SO YOU CAN SEE HOW IT WORKS. ↓

ARITHMETIC SQUARE ANSWERS PAGE 151

PLACE THE NUMBERS 1 THROUGH 9 only one time each into the nine empty cream boxes, so that they add up to the sums given at both the vertical and horizontal ends of the puzzle. Think about what numbers must fit where. Hint: Start at the top. Which three numbers must add up to make 6 in the first row?

NUMBER EQUATIONS ANSWERS PAGE 151

EACH FRUIT IS A STAND-IN for a particular number. Can you work out the value of each item of fruit, given the following picture equations?

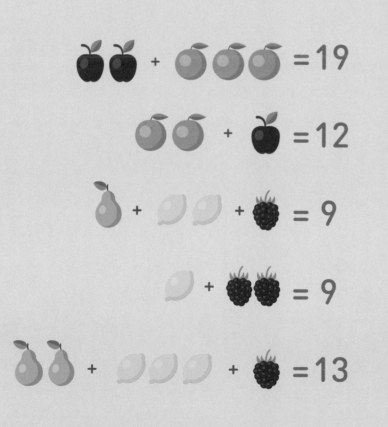

ANSWER →

ANSWER →

ANSWER →

ANSWER →

ANSWER →

COIN PUZZLES
ANSWERS PAGE 151

IN THE UNITED STATES, THERE ARE FOUR VALUES of coin that people use on a regular basis: 1¢, 5¢, 10¢, and 25¢. Assuming you have as many of each of these coins as you need, answer the following questions:

What is the minimum number of coins you need to make up a total of 88¢?

ANSWER →

If I pay $1 for something costing 63¢, what is the minimum number of coins I can receive in change?

ANSWER →

FLOATING NUMBERS
ANSWERS PAGE 151

CAN YOU FIGURE OUT HOW TO FORM each of the given totals, adding together only combinations of the six numbers given? You cannot use a number more than once in a single total.

12   10

11   7

6   4

Totals:

20 ANSWER →

30 ANSWER →

35 ANSWER →

FENCES ANSWERS PAGE 151

CONNECT EVERY DOT UNTIL YOU'VE FORMED A SINGLE LOOP. Use only horizontal and vertical lines between points, and the loop cannot cross over or touch either itself or the large blue obstacles. Some of the dots are joined already.

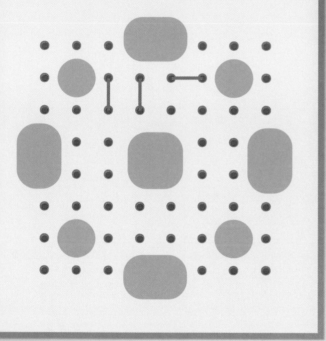

LATIN SQUARE ANSWERS PAGE 151

PLACE A NUMBER FROM 1 TO 6 into each empty square in the grid so that no number repeats in any row or column.

		1	3		
	1			2	
1		6	5		4
5		3	2		1
	3			4	
		4	6		

TOUCHY NUMBERS ANSWERS PAGE 151

PLACE A NUMBER FROM 1 TO 6 into each empty square in the grid so that no number repeats in any row or column. Sound like the previous puzzle? Sort of, but there's a catch: The same number cannot be in two touching squares, including diagonally touching squares.

				6	
				1	2
5	4				
	6				

INEQUALITY PUZZLE ANSWERS PAGE 151

PLACE A NUMBER FROM 1 TO 5 into each empty square in the grid so that no number repeats in any row or column. Here's the twist: The greater-than and less-than signs between some squares mean that the number placed in one square must be greater than or less than the number placed in another.

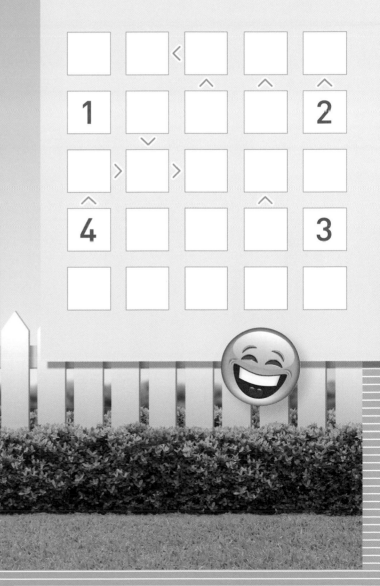

ONES AND ZEROS ANSWERS PAGE 151

PLACE 0 OR 1 INTO EACH EMPTY SQUARE of this puzzle, so that there are never more than two 0s or two 1s together in any row or column. Also, there should be exactly three 0s and three 1s in each row and column.

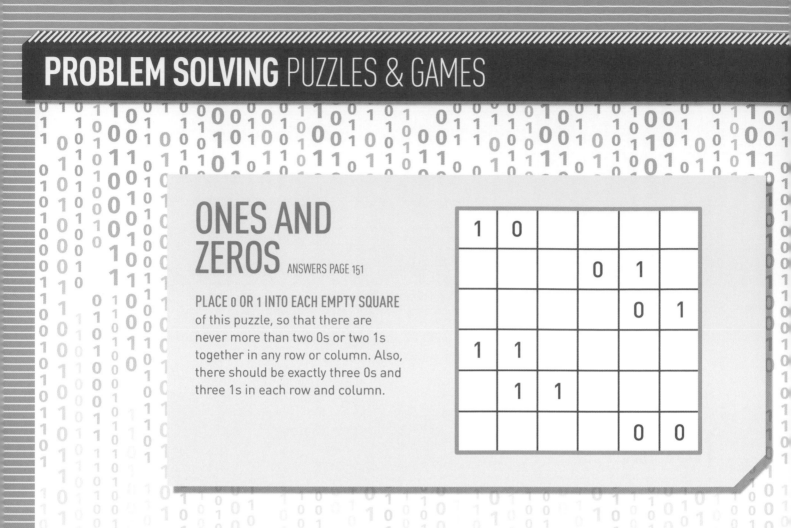

PATHFINDER ANSWERS PAGE 151

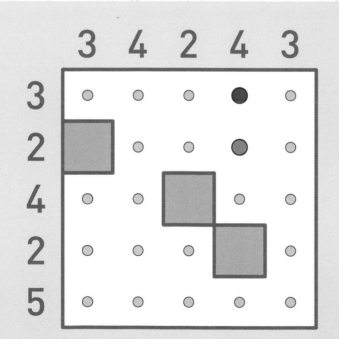

STARTING AT THE RED DOT and ending at the blue dot, draw a single path through some of the gray dots that does not touch itself or cross itself at any point. Use horizontal and vertical lines only (no diagonals), and do not cross over any of the green squares. The numbers around the outside of the grid are the total number of dots in that row or column that your path must visit, including the starting red dot and ending blue dot.

NUMBER JOURNEY ANSWERS PAGE 152

COMPLETE THE GRID so that each number from 1 to 36 appears one time. When your grid is filled, you must be able to trace a path from square 1 to square 36 in numerical order, moving only one square at a time—left, right, up, or down, but not diagonally—between touching squares. The path must visit each square only once.

1					36
		6	33		
	8	7	32	31	
	11	12	13	26	
		15	14		
18					23

KING'S JOURNEY ANSWERS PAGE 152

COMPLETE THE GRID so that each number from 1 to 25 appears only once. When the grid is completed, you must be able to trace a path from square 1 to square 25 in numerical order, moving only one square at a time like a king in chess—left, right, up, down, or diagonally—between touching squares. The path must visit each square exactly once.

		20		
23			19	
25		6		14
	1	7		13
2			9	10

MINIATURE SUDOKU ANSWERS PAGE 152

TEST OUT YOUR SUDOKU SKILLS by placing the numbers 1 to 4 once each into every row, column, and bold-lined 2x2 box of each of these four miniature sudoku puzzles.

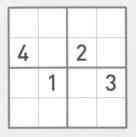

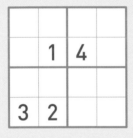

JIGSAW LETTERS ANSWERS PAGE 152

TEST OUT YOUR SUDOKU SKILLS by placing the letters A to E once each into every row, column, and bold-lined jigsaw piece shape.

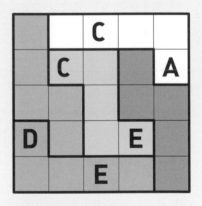

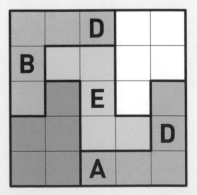

3-D SUDOKU ANSWERS PAGE 152

THIS PUZZLE FEATURES A 3-D TWIST on sudoku! Place the numbers 1 to 8 once each into every row, column, or red-lined region. The rows and columns each bend around one corner of the puzzle, so there are more than there might appear to be at first glance.

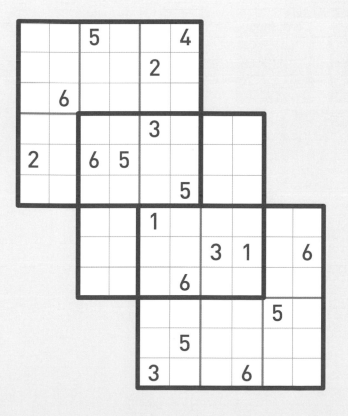

SAMURAI SUDOKU ANSWERS PAGE 152

CAN YOU PLACE THE NUMBERS 1 to 6 once each into every row, column, and blue-lined box of these three overlapping sudoku grids? Don't be tempted to solve one red-bordered grid at a time; the three grids must be solved simultaneously to reach the unique solution.

NUMBER PYRAMID ANSWERS PAGE 152

COMPLETE THE NUMBER PYRAMID BY WRITING A NUMBER IN EACH EMPTY SQUARE. Every square in the pyramid must contain a value exactly equal to the total of the two squares immediately beneath it.

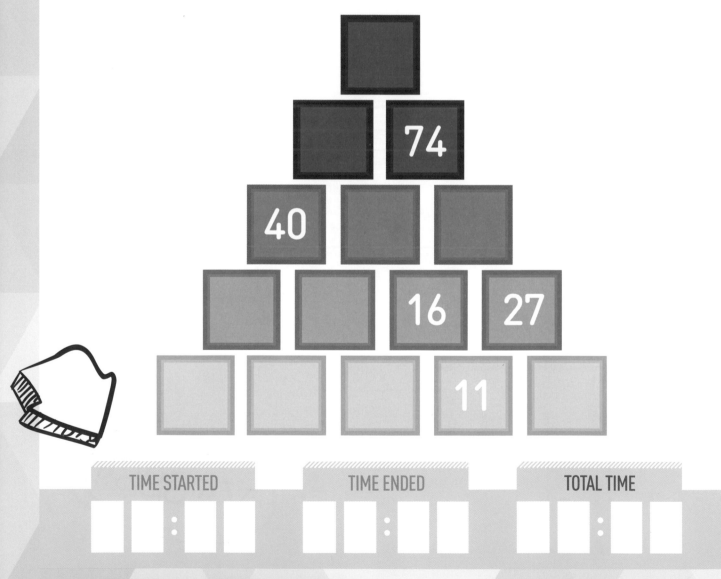

TIME STARTED	TIME ENDED	TOTAL TIME

SIMPLE LOOP ANSWERS PAGE 152

DRAW A SINGLE CLOSED LOOP THAT VISITS EVERY WHITE SQUARE EXACTLY ONCE AND CROSSES NO BLUE SQUARES.
The loop can consist of only horizontal and vertical lines and cannot cross over or touch itself in any way.

TIME STARTED

TIME ENDED

TOTAL TIME

CHAPTER SIX

BRAIN MYSTERIES

TRY THIS: Stand up. Now spin in a circle. While you're doing that, sing the ABC's.

Easy, right? Not so fast. To perform that sequence of actions, your brain had to make many adjustments all at once—too many to count. The muscles in your arms, legs, feet, and head had to work together in perfect harmony to keep you spinning without toppling over. At the same time, your memory had to recall your ABC's, while your vocal cords and mouth worked together to sing. Each of these actions required its own series of messages from the brain. And you did it all without really thinking about it. Sound like a head-scratcher? Let's uncover some of your brain's coolest mysteries.

→

ABC'S

ALPHABETICAL NUMBER SORT

WHAT COULD BE EASIER THAN SORTING SOME WORDS INTO ALPHABETICAL ORDER? Well, what if those words were numbers? Do you think it would be any tougher?

Start by sorting these 10 words into alphabetical order; write 1 to 10 above them to indicate their position in the order. Time yourself with a stopwatch and make a note of your time.

WORD SET A

PLAY   TRIUMPH   ENTIRE   WHOLE   AARDVARK

THOUGHT   WONDER   PRETEND   NONSENSE   TOOL

MY TIME WAS:

Now try with this set of numbers instead, sorting them into alphabetical order as you did above:

WORD SET B

FOUR   NINE   TWO   SIX   EIGHT

THREE   SEVEN   TEN   ONE   FIVE

MY TIME WAS:

[BEHIND THE BRAIN]

Were you slower sorting word set B? If not, congratulations! Most people are, because the fact that the words are also numbers makes it harder for our brains to think about ordering them alphabetically. Your brain is so used to thinking about numbers in terms of their values, which themselves have a very precise ordering (1, 2, 3 ...), that it finds it hard to ignore that existing ordering when you then try to sort them alphabetically instead.

YOUR HIDDEN BRAIN

PIONEERING PSYCHOLOGIST SIGMUND FREUD ONCE COMPARED THE MIND TO AN ICEBERG:

Above the surface is the conscious mind, or your thoughts and perception of the world around you. But most of the mind lies underneath: This is the unconscious, the part of your mind you're not aware of. When you swim, play the piano, or read a book, most of the action seems automatic. But each task involves countless messages zipping around your neurons.

Because so much of the brain's activity occurs below the surface, it's challenging for neuroscientists to unravel exactly what's going on in there. They can zap the brain with electrodes and map it with MRI scans, but some secrets of your skull have them stumped ... for now.

MENTAL MYSTERIES

Here are some of the questions that have brain scientists scratching their heads.

→ What is the language of the brain?
In the beginning of this book, you learned that neurons in the brain use electrical signals to send messages to each other. But how do these signals communicate meaning? In other words, what language are they speaking? One theory is that it's the location of the electrical signals in the brain that conveys meaning.

But since each neuron communicates with about 10,000 others, it's nearly impossible to track their paths.

→ How are memories stored?
Humans have two types of memory—short-term, which you use when you hold a sentence in your head long enough to write it down, and long-term, which you use when you recall the plot of your favorite movie. But how does the brain decide what information to save? And why can't you recall some memories when you need them? Despite lots of studies, much about your memory remains a mystery.

→ Why do we sleep?
We spend one-third of our lives snoozing, but the reason why is still kind of a mystery. Scientists have learned that we need sleep to survive, of course: Not getting enough makes us more likely to get sick, and severe sleep deprivation can cause hallucinations and even death. So for a while, scientists thought sleep was when the body rested and restored itself. But then they found out that the brain is extremely active during sleep. Scientists now think that sleep is crucial to learning ... but they're not sure how.

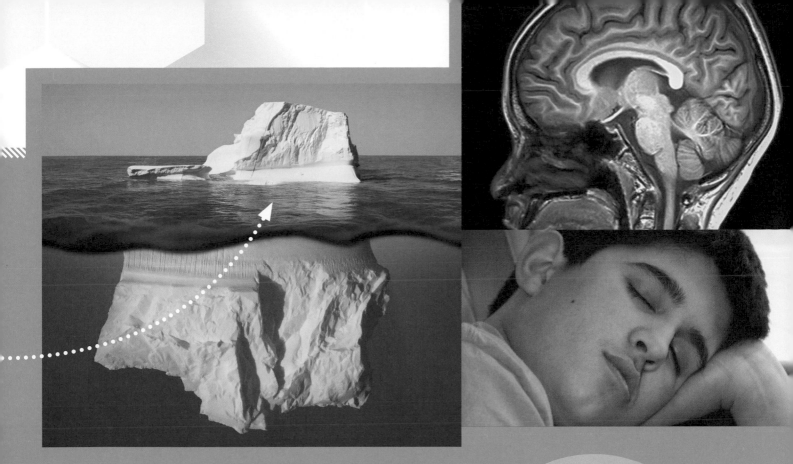

→ What are dreams?

One second, you're resting comfortably on your pillow. The next, you're riding a kangaroo alongside your school principal. It's a dream—but what is the purpose of this bizarre brain activity? Most dreams happen during a phase of sleep called REM (rapid eye movement). During REM sleep, the body's muscles become temporarily paralyzed. Breathing and heart rate become irregular, and brain activity spikes. Some scientists think the dreams you have during this stage are your brain's way of hitting the gym—running through potential solutions to problems and deciding which thoughts to store as memories.

YOUR **BRAIN** CAN BE JUST AS **ACTIVE** WHEN YOU'RE **ASLEEP** AS IT IS WHEN YOU'RE **AWAKE.**

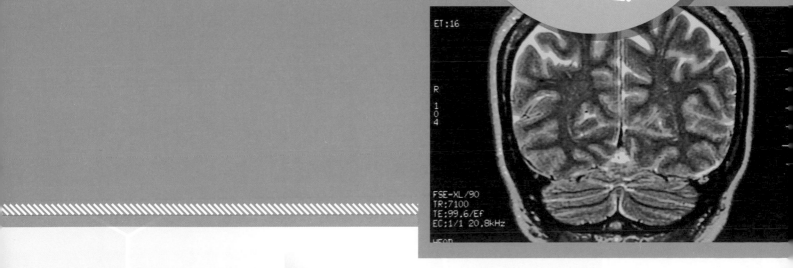

ET:16

R 104

FSE-XL/90
TR:7100
TE:99.6/Ef
EC:1/1 20.8kHz

JUMBLED WORDS ANSWERS PAGE 153

WHEN THE LETTERS IN A WORD ARE ALL MIXED UP, it's pretty hard to read the results. Try this sentence, for example:

IHTS AXLEMEP SI UTIQE TLUFIDIFC OT DEAR

But when you start each word with the correct letter, it suddenly gets a bit easier:

TIHS EXLAMEP IS QUTIE DLUFIIFCT TO RDEA

CAN YOU READ IT NOW?
This works for any sentence, as long as none of the words are too long. The reason is because we often retrieve words via their first letter from our memories. You may have experienced this as the "tip of the tongue" effect, in which you are sure you know the first letter of something but can't recall the entire word!

INVERTED WORDS ANSWERS PAGE 153

THE HUMAN BRAIN IS GOOD AT READING. It's so good it can even make sense of letters when all you can see is some of the background around them and not the letters or the edge of the word at all. For example, try reading this word:

Even though the start and end of the first and last letters are missing, along with all the tops and bottoms of the letters, we bet you can still read it.

SHADOW WORDS ANSWERS PAGE 153

WE BET YOU CAN EVEN READ A WORD WHEN YOU CAN SEE **JUST** A SHADOW OF EACH LETTER.
Your brain fills in the rest, making it surprisingly simple to read:

CLIMATE

OVERLAID WORDS ANSWERS PAGE 153

THIS PICTURE LOOKS LIKE A MESS OF OVERLAID LETTERS AND COLORS AT FIRST GLANCE:

But look closer and you may surprise yourself. Study it for a few moments, and then try to make out the dark red letters. Can you read the word?

Now study the light green letters: Can you read what they say, too?

It might take a bit of concentration, but you'll probably find that you can suddenly see the word you are looking at pretty clearly. Amazing!

FACE CONFUSION

HAVE A LOOK AT THESE TWO FACES. Apart from the one on the right being upside down, nothing seems unusual, does it?

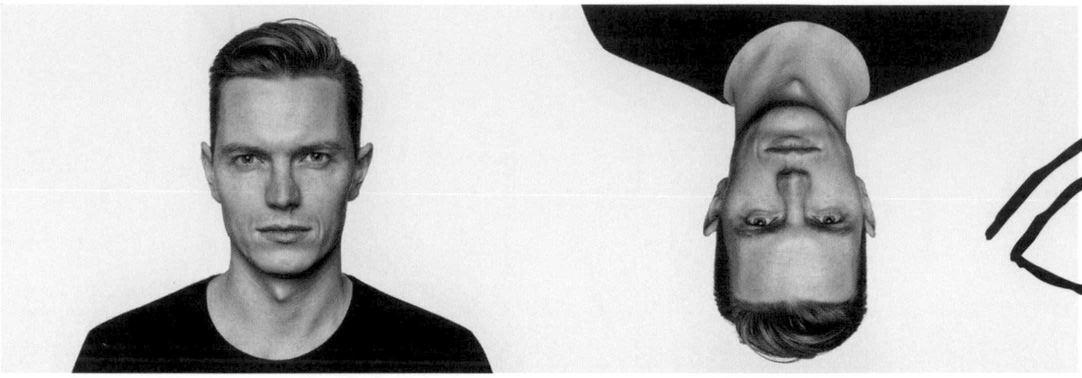

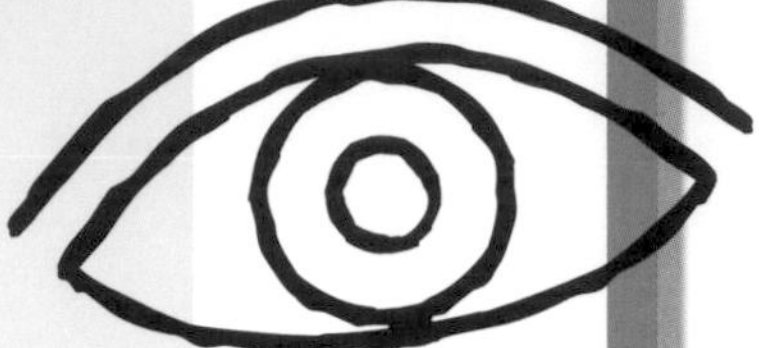

Are you sure? Try turning the page upside down.

[BEHIND THE BRAIN]

In the image on the right, the head is upside down but the eyes and mouth are still right-side up. In normal life you rarely encounter anyone whose head is the wrong way up, so your brain isn't particularly experienced at identifying upside-down faces and so doesn't notice the problem. But what your brain is very good at is spotting faces (as you'll see again on the next page), so it has no trouble identifying the image as a face.

VISUAL CONFUSION

ANSWERS PAGE 153

TAKE A LOOK AT THESE SEEMINGLY RANDOM CHARACTERS: Not much to see here, right? But put the book down, propping it up so that you can see this page from across the room, and go as far away as you can before looking back. What do you see now?

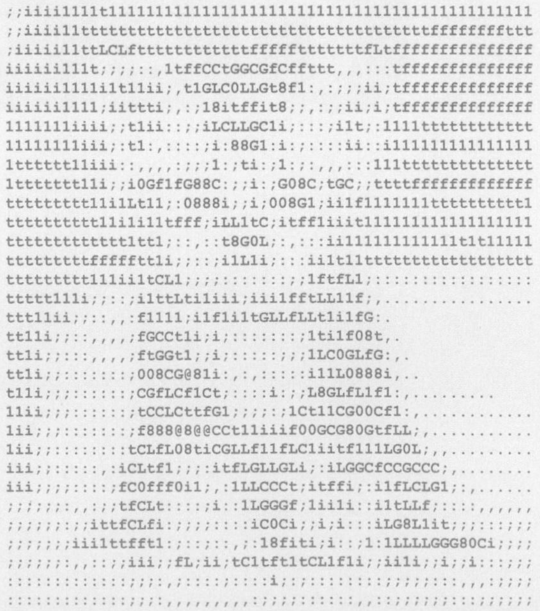

HIDDEN FACES

SO POWERFUL IS THE BRAIN'S FACE-SPOTTING ABILITY THAT WE CAN EVEN SEE FACES WHERE WE KNOW THERE DEFINITELY AREN'T ANY! Can you find anything familiar in the following pictures?

DOES THIS DOUBLE FIRE HYDRANT SEEM TO BE LOOKING BACK AT YOU?

HOW ABOUT THIS TREE?

DOES THIS TRACTOR SPORT A SERIOUS EXPRESSION?

IS THIS CUTTING TOOL SHOWING A SIDEWAYS SMILE?

COUNT COMPARISON

WITHOUT ACTUALLY COUNTING (AND WITHOUT READING THIS PUZZLE'S BEHIND THE BRAIN!), glance quickly at the picture below and decide which shape there are most of, which shape there are second most of, and which shape appears the least. Make a note of your guesses below.

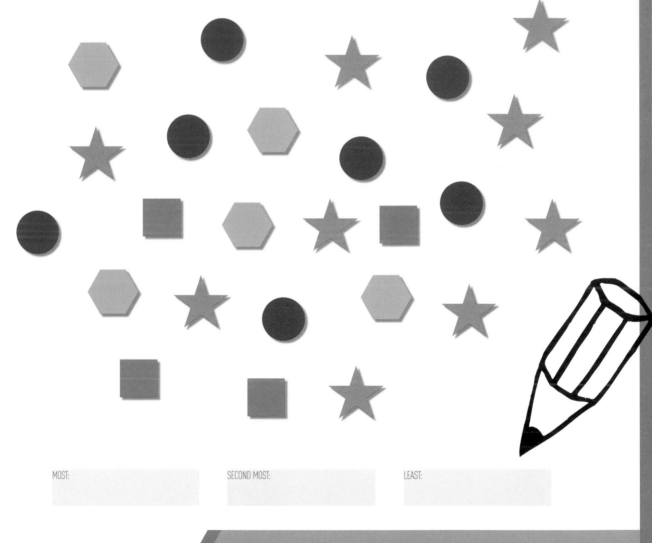

MOST:

SECOND MOST:

LEAST:

[BEHIND THE BRAIN]

There are more gold stars than any other shape; did you notice that immediately? There are nine of them. Next up, there are seven red circles, five green hexagons, and, finally, four blue squares. That's a total of 25 shapes, and yet your brain was able to immediately process what you were looking at and give you a rapid estimate of how frequently each shape appeared. This ability might not be that useful nowadays, but back in hunter-gatherer times it would have allowed you to rapidly size up your chances against various groups of animals, so you could take the safest escape route!

ROUNDING AND ESTIMATION ANSWERS PAGE 153

HAVE YOU EVER GONE AROUND A SUPERMARKET AND TRIED TO KEEP TRACK OF THE TOTAL VALUE OF WHAT WAS BEING PUT INTO YOUR SHOPPING CART?
It's tricky to keep an exact count, but usually all you'd ever need is a rough estimate of the total; that way, when you get to the checkout, it doesn't come as a complete surprise once you start paying the bill!

The great thing about working out totals of this kind is that you deliberately don't worry about getting them exactly right. Just keep track of the number of dollars and forget the cents: If the price ends in 50 cents or higher, round up to the nearest number of dollars; if it ends in 49 cents or lower, just ignore the cents. For example, for a price of $12.55 you would round up and to $13, but for a price of $12.45 you would round down to only $12.

Over all the items you buy, the inaccuracies tend to average out, meaning the final total is usually more or less correct.

Try it with these shopping items. What estimated total do you get using this method?

| $3.55 | $4.83 | $2.35 | $9.95 | $11.30 | $6.40 |
| $8.30 | $2.22 | $7.78 | $4.40 | $3.35 | $7.55 |

MY ESTIMATED TOTAL IS: $

MAGICAL MULTIPLES

DID YOU KNOW THAT YOU CAN TELL ALMOST IMMEDIATELY IF ANY GIVEN NUMBER IS A MULTIPLE OF THREE, no matter how big the number?

Take this number:
384,732,345

You probably have no clue off the bat whether it's a multiple of three. But if you were to use a calculator or work it out with long division, you'd find that it is in fact equal to 3 x 128,244,115.

However, if you simply **add up** the digits of any number and the resulting total is a multiple of three, then **so is the original number!**

So, 3 + 8 + 4 + 7 + 3 + 2 + 3 + 4 + 5 = 39. You know that 39 is equal to 3 x 13. Therefore, the original number **is** a multiple of three.

This works for any number—try it! And if the total is **both** even **and** a multiple of three, then the original number is a multiple of six, too!

IMAGE MEMORY ANSWERS PAGE 153

COVER THE BOTTOM HALF OF THIS PAGE AND TAKE A QUICK SCAN THROUGH THE PICTURES ON THE TOP HALF OF THE PAGE FOR AROUND 30 SECONDS OR SO.

Next, remove the cover from the bottom half of the page and use it to cover the top half of the page instead. Then, circle the pictures you have seen before.

Once you are finished, check back to the original image to see how many you got right and make a note of the result. Subtract one from your total for any you incorrectly circled.

Did you get more than you expected? Your brain is very good at remembering pictures, even if you only see them once and quite briefly. If this page had been full of numbers instead, you would have been much less likely to remember so many!

MEMORY PALACES

REMEMBERING PICTURES YOU'VE SEEN BEFORE IS SOMETHING YOUR BRAIN EXCELS AT.

For example, if you are given a pile of photographs to look through, you can probably easily identify most of those that you have seen before.

Remembering items in general is much trickier, however. One method for memorizing lists is called the memory palace technique, and it works by imagining a route around a building you are very familiar with, such as your home or school. It works best if the building has a lot of rooms.

To use the technique, you start by deciding on a fixed route you will always follow through the building. Then you imagine walking that route and placing each item you want to remember in one of the rooms. The more ridiculous the association between the item and the room, the more memorable it will be! This is because things that are out of the ordinary seem more important to your brain, so it makes note of them more easily. Anything more normal is generally quickly forgotten, which is why you probably don't remember every detail of what you did yesterday; your brain considers it so unremarkable that it doesn't bother remembering it. Unusual events, such as your first day at a new school, are by comparison much more memorable.

For example, say your route is that you go into a hall, through a living room, into a kitchen, and then back out onto some stairs before traveling into a bedroom. This palace has five rooms, so you can use it to confidently remember five items. Say those items are a grocery list:

BREAD	MILK	APPLES	JUICE	BUTTER

You might then remember them as follows:
- I go into the hall, where the carpet is made out of slices of bread.
- I enter the living room, which has milk cartons instead of light fixtures.
- I enter the kitchen, but the faucets have been replaced with apples.
- I go onto the stairs, but they are slippery because juice is pouring down them.
- I enter the bedroom, but somebody has spread my sheets with butter!

Your trip through the building never changes, so you only need to learn it once. Then, once you've learned it, you can use it as many times as you like, for any set of items you want to remember. And if you ever need to remember more items than you have rooms, you can simply add on as many rooms as you need. These don't need to be real rooms, so if you want a swimming pool room, then you can have one!

Let's see if you can remember the five items without having made any conscious effort to memorize them. Here are the rooms; can you remember which grocery item was in each room?

1) Hall   _____
2) Living room   _____
3) Kitchen   _____
4) Stairs   _____
5) Bedroom   _____

If you remember most, or even all, of the items, then congratulations! Build up your memory palace and you can start to demonstrate impressive memory skills.

MISSING WORDS ANSWERS PAGE 153

COVER THE BOTTOM SET OF WORDS, and then study the top list for as long as you like. Then cover over the top list and see if you can identify which three words that were in the top are missing from the bottom.

DOG	WATER	STREAM	DINOSAUR
TYPEFACE	CLEVER	DREAMER	BONUS
UNIQUE	ELEMENT	GEOGRAPHY	CLOUD
DOUGHNUT	FANTASTIC	REFERENCE	BASEBALL

BASEBALL	BONUS	CLEVER	CLOUD
DINOSAUR	DOG	DOUGHNUT	ELEMENT
FANTASTIC	GEOGRAPHY	STREAM	TYPEFACE
WATER	_____	_____	_____

How did you do? You might have found it harder than the image memory task on the previous page. You can ask other people to make more tests like the one above for you, if you want to practice more.

SHAPE ORDER ANSWERS PAGE 153

REMEMBERING THE ORDER OF ITEMS IN A LIST IS ONE OF THE BENEFITS OF USING THE MEMORY PALACE TECHNIQUE YOU LEARNED ABOUT ON THE PREVIOUS PAGE. Start by covering the bottom row of shapes. Then, either by using the memory palace method or any technique you like, try to remember the order of the shapes in the top row. Once you think you are ready, uncover the bottom row and cover the top row of shapes instead. Now, number the shapes in the second list in the order you think they appeared in the first list.

How did you do? You might have found this trickier than you expected. Remembering an order, especially for abstract shapes, can be difficult!

WORD SEARCH MEMORY

ANSWERS PAGE 153

SPEND A FEW MINUTES ATTEMPTING TO MEMORIZE THIS LIST OF WORDS. They are all shades of colors.

ALMOND   CHAMPAGNE   MUSTARD
AMBER   CINNAMON   OLD GOLD
BEIGE   DAFFODIL   PRIMROSE
BISQUE   EGGSHELL   TOPAZ
BUFF   GOLDEN
BUTTERNUT   MAGNOLIA

Now, cover the list and—without peeking—see how many you can find in this word search. Words can be written in any direction: diagonally, forward, or backward.

```
I L L E H S G G E D M
F T O P A Z C R U L A
B F C N R A H D Q O G
T U U I M I A T S G N
N M T B N F M C I D O
D E E T F N P R B L L
N R D O E E A I O O I
O N D L E R G M D S A
M I L S O A N I O F E
L E N A O G E U E N O
A M U S T A R D T B L
```

You might find that the word search grid helps you remember more words than you otherwise would by helping you locate the first one or two letters to jog your memory as you search.

NO FOUR IN A ROW

ANSWERS PAGE 153

FILL IN THIS GRID SO THAT EVERY SQUARE CONTAINS EITHER AN *O* OR AN *X*. You must place these so that there are no rows of four (or more) *O*'s or *X*'s in any direction, including diagonally.

If you get stuck, try making a guess in pencil and see if it works out; experimentation is a great way to make progress on a problem. Be sure to keep track of what that guess was (and what you placed afterward) so that you can undo the guess if it turns out to be wrong.

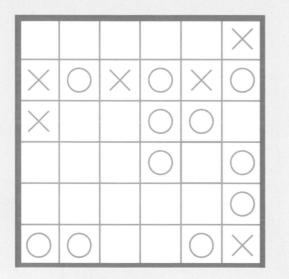

MINDSWEEPER ANSWERS PAGE 153

MINES ARE HIDDEN IN SOME OF THE EMPTY SQUARES IN THIS GRID. Luckily, you can figure out exactly where they are by using the number clues. Each number tells you exactly how many mines there are in the touching squares surrounding each number, which includes diagonally touching squares.

Can you find all the mines? Again, if you get stuck, making a good guess and seeing how it works out can be a useful technique!

HERE'S AN EXAMPLE OF A SOLVED PUZZLE SO YOU CAN SEE HOW THE NUMBERS RELATE TO THE TOUCHING MINES. →

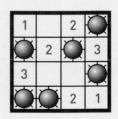

1	2			1	
	2				0
2	2			1	1
	2		1		1
3		3		2	1
2					

PIXEL ART

JUST AS GUESSING CAN BE A GOOD TECHNIQUE FOR GETTING GOING AGAIN WHEN YOU GET STUCK ON A PUZZLE, making random "guesses" can be useful for creative processes, too. Start here by randomly shading in several squares in this grid with colored pens or pencils, and then step back: What does it look like? Anything at all, or just some dots? Shade some more, and try again. Once you think you can "see" what the image might look like, keep shading until you have completed a simple picture or pattern.

COLORING PATTERNS

JUST LIKE IN THE PREVIOUS ACTIVITY, grab some colored pens or pencils and color in a few areas in this picture without much thought. Take a step back and see what you have made so far: Does it look like anything, or could you develop it into a pattern? Continue until you decide you've finished ... and then congratulate yourself on the art you just made!

JOIN THE DOTS

IT'S TIME TO CONNECT SOME DOTS ... but not to create a specific picture: Make anything you like!

Use only straight lines to join pairs of dots. As you start to draw, you may find that a picture starts to appear—perhaps a face, or a bird, or a star constellation. Not all dots have to be connected, and you could even leave some of them to act as "eyes" within a face.

WHAT'S IN THE BOX?

HERE ARE TWO BLANK BOXES, each with something sticking out of them. Use your imagination to draw what's inside the box. There's no correct answer—it's entirely up to you!

IMAGINE

EXPLAIN THIS!

CAN YOU EXPLAIN WHAT EACH OF THESE PICTURES SHOWS? Use your imagination and be as creative as you like. For example, perhaps the first picture is a polar bear in the snow, and you can only see his nose.

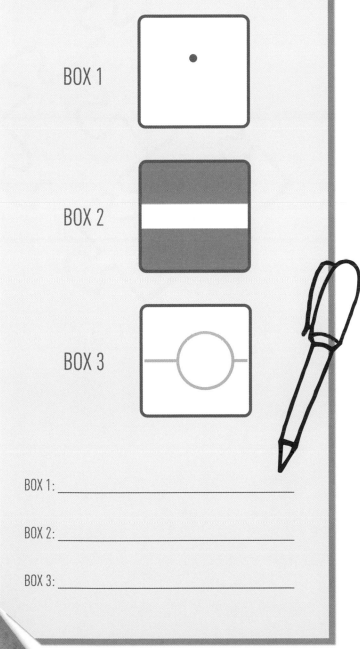

BOX 1

BOX 2

BOX 3

BOX 1: _____

BOX 2: _____

BOX 3: _____

TANGRAMS ANSWERS PAGE 153

TRACE THIS SQUARE AND ITS INTERNAL LINES ONTO ANOTHER PIECE OF PAPER. Color each shape according to how it is colored in the box below. Then cut out each of the seven shapes. Congratulations—you have created yourself a "tangram" set!

The tangram is an ancient puzzle that was invented in China more than 1,000 years ago and brought to the West during the early 19th century. The aim is to rearrange the tangram pieces to form as many different pictures as you can. There's just one rule: The pieces should not overlap, and you can't turn them over to show the uncolored side.

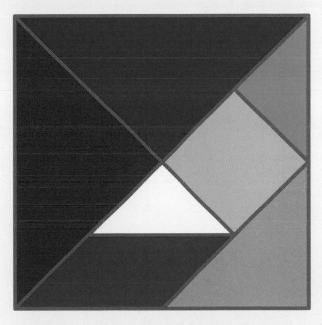

Can you figure out how to rearrange them to make a dog, so the overall shape looks like this? The solution is in the back of the book, in case you get stuck!

Use your tangrams to make more pictures like a swan, candlestick, cat, house, boat—or even a chair!

COMPLETE THE LIMERICK

USE YOUR CREATIVE WRITING SKILLS TO COMPLETE THIS PARTIALLY FINISHED LIMERICK. The first, second, and fifth lines should rhyme. And the third and fourth lines should rhyme, too. It doesn't matter what you write, but limericks work best when they're silly.

THERE WAS AN OLD MAN FROM _____

WHOSE _____ WAS AS GREEN AS A _____

HE FELL FROM A _____

AFTER TRYING TO _____

AND ENDED UP STUCK IN THE _____

IT'S YOUR JOKE

HERE ARE SOME JOKES ... except that, in each case, the punch line is missing! Can you fill in the blank line with an amusing response? There are no correct answers: It's up to you to be creative!

WHY DID THE ARMADILLO CROSS THE ROAD?

_____

WHAT DO YOU CALL A CELEBRITY WHO'S NO LONGER FAMOUS?

_____

WHAT GOES "BOING, BOING, BOING" WHILE FALLING DOWN STAIRS?

_____

POETIC LICENSE

THESE SHORT TWO-LINE POEMS ARE ALL MISSING THEIR SECOND LINES. Can you write a concluding sentence for each poem, making sure that both lines rhyme?

IN TIME GONE BY I USED TO THINK,

_____

ONCE THERE WAS A WIZARD DO, WITH WIZARD HATS AND WIZARDS WHO,

_____

MELLOW MUSIC FLOATS AROUND,

_____

SOME REARRANGEMENT NECESSARY

SOMETIMES IT'S ACTUALLY **EASIER** TO WRITE WHEN THERE ARE RULES, because it helps remove the "I don't know where to start" feeling that can make it tricky to get going! Grab a piece of paper and a pencil, and see if you can write a very short and simple story using the words listed here. In some sentences, is it possible to use only these words and no others? Try it!

THE	ON	THAT	SAID	CAT	FOREST	LEAF	BREAD
IN	BY	HAVE	JUST	DOG	TREES	WIND	HOME
OF	FOR	IT	KNOW	MUSIC	WHERE	STRONG	
AND	FROM	HE	HAD	STRANGE	HEARD	END	
A	TO	SHE	AT	CLEVER	PLAYING	CAME	
AN	WITH	THEM	WAS	WALK	EVERY	CHEESE	

TiME TRiALS

NUMBER PYRAMID ANSWERS PAGE 153

COMPLETE THE NUMBER PYRAMID BY WRITING A NUMBER IN EACH EMPTY SQUARE. Every square in the pyramid must contain a value exactly equal to the total of the two squares immediately beneath it.

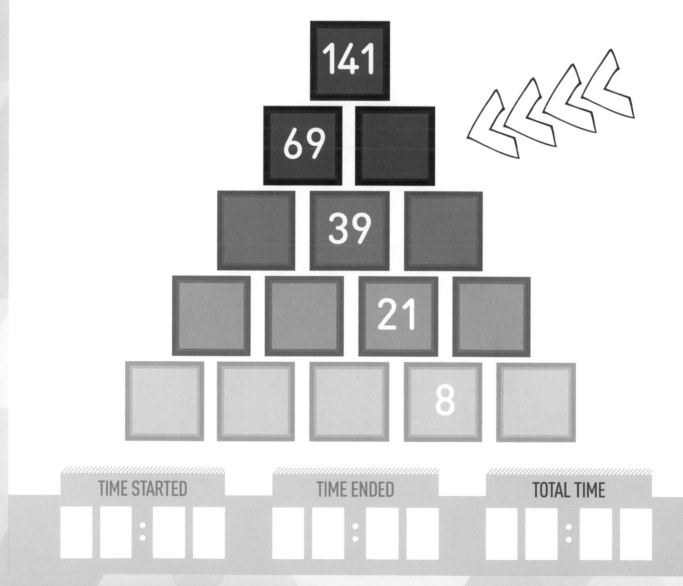

TIME STARTED	TIME ENDED	TOTAL TIME
☐☐ : ☐☐	☐☐ : ☐☐	☐☐ : ☐☐

SIMPLE LOOP ANSWERS PAGE 153

DRAW A SINGLE CLOSED LOOP THAT VISITS EVERY WHITE SQUARE EXACTLY ONCE AND CROSSES NO BLUE SQUARES.
The loop can consist of only horizontal and vertical lines and cannot cross over or touch itself in any way.

TIME STARTED

TIME ENDED

TOTAL TIME

CHAPTER SEVEN

ANIMAL INTELLIGENCE

YOUR DOG KNOWS HOW TO SIT ON COMMAND. He knows where his leash is hanging and somehow can even sense when he's about to get a bath. But is Fido truly intelligent?

For a long time, people thought *Homo sapiens* were the only smart species on the planet. But research over the past few decades has turned that old idea on its head. We now know that Earth is brimming with brainy beasts.

Animal intelligence is easy to recognize when it's similar to our own. When we see a chimpanzee using tools to get honey out of a bee's nest, or a gorilla communicating with sign language, we see intelligence. But it's harder to see the signs of smarts in animals that are totally different from us. Let's meet a few unexpected animal geniuses.

$\rightarrow$

FLYING SQUIRREL **COMPETITION**

JUST AS WE HUMANS HAVE MANY AMAZING ABILITIES (many of which you've explored elsewhere in this book!), the animal kingdom is also full of incredible skills. For example, the flying squirrel has one of the strangest abilities: This mammal has evolved to have long flaps of skin between its arms and its torso; these flaps allow it to glide from the tops of trees without plummeting to the forest floor far below. Handy!

You can't glide, of course, but you *could* try making gliders out of sheets of paper. If you have any scrap paper, now's a good chance to use it!

Start each glider by taking a piece of paper and folding and unfolding along the middle of the sheet of paper to make a crease, as shown in picture 1. Next, fold two opposite corners down into the crease, as shown in picture 2, to result in picture 3. Next, fold the same corners into the center again, because you're making the nose of your glider and you don't want it to be too light; this is shown in pictures 4 and 5. Finally, fold the paper in half along the original crease, and fold down the wings on either side (picture 6). The result is shown in picture 7—and that's your glider! Throw it gently. How far does it glide?

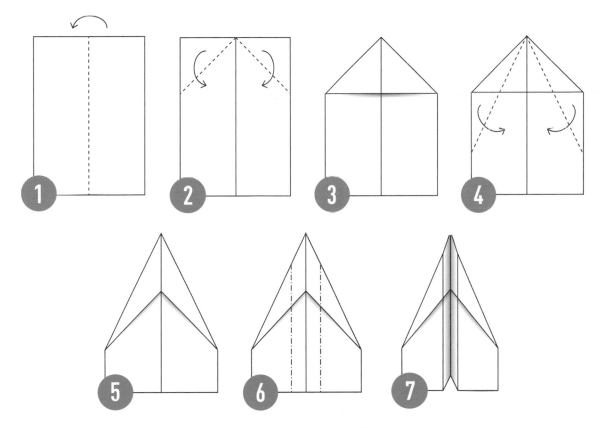

You can experiment to see if you can make it go farther by adjusting some of the folds to shift the weight balance. You could also try folding the paper the other way in the first step, so you fold along the shorter length of the rectangle.

Another option is to try tearing small flaps in the paper at the tail of the plane, and then folding these up or down. This will alter the way it flies through the air, making the nose push up (if you fold the flaps up) or push down (if you fold the flaps down). A flying squirrel will make small adjustments to its "wings" as it flies through the air to control its path, but with your glider you have to make all the adjustments before you throw it!

CRAFTY CREATURES

WITH THEIR SUCKERED ARMS AND W-SHAPED PUPILS, CUTTLEFISH—A TYPE OF SEA CREATURE CALLED A CEPHALOPOD—ALMOST SEEM LIKE ALIENS. BUT EVEN THOUGH THEY LOOK TOTALLY DIFFERENT FROM HUMANS, WE NOW KNOW THAT THEY'RE ONE OF THE SMARTEST ANIMALS ON THE PLANET.

W-SHAPED PUPILS

ARMS & TENTACLES

FIN

CUTTLEFISH

Humans' sophisticated communication is considered a sign of our smarts—but we're not the only animals with this ability. Cuttlefish can change their colors and patterns at will. They use this snazzy skill to hide from predators—but they also use their bodies like flashing neon signs to communicate with other cuttlefish. Their language is so sophisticated that they can show a friendly display on one side of their body to a potential mate and an aggressive display on the other side to another competing male.

The octopus is another smart—and strange— cephalopod. Only one-third of its brain is inside its head—the rest is in its eight legs! These bizarre brainiacs can navigate mazes, open jars, and decorate their dens with shells. Scientists who study them swear they even have individual personalities. One legendary octopus at the Brighton Aquarium in England snuck out of its tank at night when no one was watching, climbed into the tank next door, ate the fish inside, and went back to his own tank. It took the aquarium workers a while to figure out why their fish were disappearing!

BRIGHT BEES

Tiny insects can't possibly be intelligent ... or can they? Recent studies have found that honeybees—even though their brain is no bigger than a pinhead—can count to four, recognize faces, and even be trained to tell a Picasso painting from one by Monet. Scientists have even taught bees to play soccer!

But even more amazing is the way bees talk to each other. When scout bees find a source of food, they'll come back to the hive and perform a "waggle dance," a series of precise moves that give their colony-mates directions to the new flower patch. With this dance, bees can communicate the distance and direction of a new food source more than three miles (5 km) away.

They can even explain how much there is to eat and whether the area is dangerous.

CRAFTY CROWS

Crows have been observed cracking walnuts by dropping them in the paths of cars, and then waiting until the vehicle's tires do the hard work for them. Not impressed? These bright birds wait to swoop in and retrieve the food until the light is red and the crosswalk sign is on, so they don't get run over.

In 2008, a group of scientists in Seattle, Washington, U.S.A., decided to find out exactly how smart crows are. Researchers put on caveman masks and then trapped seven crows on a college campus and put bands on their legs. Months later, they put the masks back on and walked around to see if the crows would remember their captors. They did: The crows made a big fuss, squawking and harassing the caveman mask-wearers. They ignored other researchers wearing different masks.

As time passed, even crows who hadn't been messed with started scolding the scientists, showing that the group that had been trapped and banded could communicate to its crow friends what had happened. It gives a whole new meaning to the term "bird brain!"

A **CROW** IS ABOUT AS **SMART** AS A SEVEN-YEAR-OLD HUMAN.

BLACK-AND-WHITE VERSUS COLOR VISION ANSWERS PAGE 154

NOT ALL ANIMALS HAVE COLOR VISION. In fact, a number are color-blind. Imagine that you had to navigate the world without being able to see certain colors ... or any colors at all. Do you think you would find it harder?

Take a look at this picture. Can you explain the different parts of the scene?

It's hard to interpret, isn't it? You might be able to make sense of the right-hand side, but the left-hand side of the photo looks strange: It doesn't seem to match up with the other side.

Once you have a theory about what the various parts of the image could be, turn to the solutions and check the color version. Were you correct?

CELLULAR VISION ANSWERS PAGE 154

IF YOU THOUGHT NOT BEING ABLE TO SEE COLORS WAS TRICKY, IMAGINE THIS: Flies see in a mosaic-like pattern of light and dark, thanks to their compound eyes. These consist of lots of tiny visual units, all pointing in slightly different directions. Their vision does have one incredible advantage, however: It is extremely quick. In fact, flies have the fastest vision in the animal kingdom and are able to react to movement as much as five times faster than a human! It all has to do with the unique way their eyes are connected to their brain.

That speedy response allows them to jump out of harm's way—most of the time, anyway. Their vision is primarily based around this speed of response, and therefore the "big picture" is less important.

Can you identify this famous location, shown how it might appear to a fly? If you have trouble, try propping the book upright and viewing it from some distance.

WRAPAROUND VISION

SOME ANIMALS CAN SEE FAR MORE OF THE WORLD THAN WE CAN. We see mostly just in front of us, with some less detailed awareness of what happens on the sides of us. A pigeon, by comparison, has a view of about 340 degrees all around, thanks to eyes mounted on the sides of its head.

A pigeon sitting on the side of a road would therefore have a view that looks something like this:

This wide view is useful both for spotting sources of food *and* avoiding predators.

There may not be predators after you, but if you have access to a camera or camera phone with the option, try taking some "panorama" images to simulate having wraparound vision like a pigeon. If you don't have a camera, try drawing a panorama of the view all around you.

Check out how these famous places would look to you if you had panoramic vision:

THE GRAND CANYON, ARIZONA, U.S.A.

TIMES SQUARE, NEW YORK CITY

BIRD OF PREY

BIRDS OF PREY HAVE INCREDIBLY POWERFUL VISION. They can look down from a great height on a large area and then "zoom in" on a small detail a long way down below! Can you imagine spotting a small animal, such as a mouse, when looking down on a scene such as this one?

You'd need a pair of binoculars and incredibly steady hands. And just imagine trying to do this while moving quickly through the sky and being knocked around by the wind!

HUMMINGBIRD HOVER POWER ANSWERS PAGE 154

HUMMINGBIRDS HAVE A REMARKABLE SKILL ALL THEIR OWN. They can hover in the same place by beating their wings up and down incredibly quickly. In fact, they need to beat their wings around 50 times a second to hover! This means they use a huge amount of energy.

Hummingbirds need to consume around five calories per day. This may not sound like a lot, but they are much smaller than humans and have a much faster heart rate, meaning they use energy faster. Relative to size, they need to consume around 75 times as many calories as we do!

Pound-for-pound, if the average human eats 2,000 calories in a day, how many calories would that average human need to consume in a single day to eat (proportionately) as much as a hummingbird?

SQUIRREL SKILLS

ANSWERS PAGE 154

MANY ANIMALS ARE ABLE TO LEARN COMPLEX ROUTINES TO FIND FOOD.
One animal that has proven to be particularly skilled at doing this is the squirrel.
Some homeowners who put nuts out for birds to eat have devised creative ways to stop local squirrels from eating them instead. The clever squirrels, however, are masters at obstacle courses and are rarely deterred: They've shown they can hang from ropes, slide down poles, climb up vertical columns, and leap incredible distances—all in the pursuit of a few nuts!
Test your squirrel skills by looking at the picture below. Which of the platforms, A or B, would you need to jump onto to make the nut drop down to where the red arrow is?

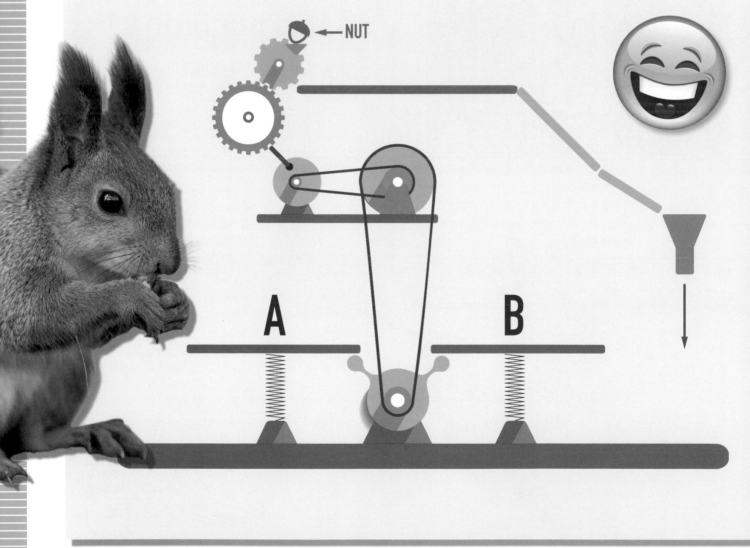

SUPER SENSE OF SMELL ANSWERS PAGE 154

DOGS HAVE AN INCREDIBLY POWERFUL SENSE OF SMELL. They can still detect the lingering odor of a person, or another dog, days after they have visited a location. They can sometimes track the exact route a particular person took.

How are your tracking skills? An animal has left the pond at the top of the picture, leaving a trail of footprints. Which one of the exit points at the bottom, labeled A to D, did they use to exit the scene?

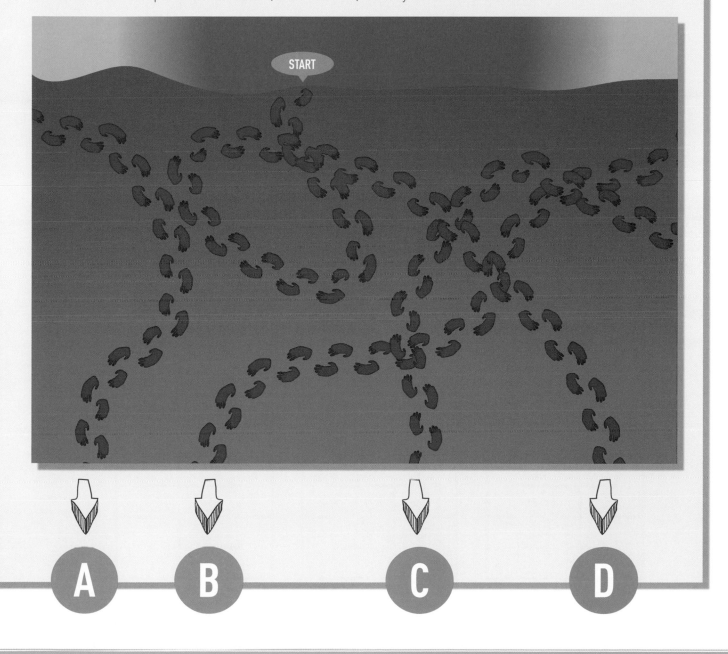

ANT PHEROMONES ANSWERS PAGE 154

SOCIAL INSECTS, SUCH AS ANTS, create colonies that behave more intelligently than any single insect does on its own. If you've ever watched ants scurry around, seemingly randomly exploring, then you probably won't think of ants as master navigators—but they are!

If you leave a sugar cube near an ant nest and come back later, you might see a perfect procession of ants, all following the same route to and from the cube. They work in harmony, often finding a direct route to their destination. How do they do this?

The secret is pheromones. Ants leave a small amount of a chemical marker behind as they explore, and other ants can smell it. The more ants that pass one way, the stronger the smell gets, and the trail gets stronger and stronger. When they find something good, they leave a stronger scent, so the ants that have found shorter, better routes reinforce the trail more than those who haven't. Over time, lots and lots of ants find a trail that gets better and better.

Want to try navigating like an ant? Check out the simple mazes below. Five ant trails are shown, running from top to bottom. On the sixth empty maze, write on each blue grid square how many ants have passed through it. For example, the top-left square is passed through by two ants, so write a 2 in that same square. And the top-middle square is passed through by all five ants, so write a 5 in that square.

Next, trace a route through that sixth maze yourself, starting at the top center square and then always moving to the neighboring square with the highest value, just as an ant tends to follow the strongest scent. Draw in the route you follow. Congratulations! You've just found a great route through the maze in just the same way that an ant would.

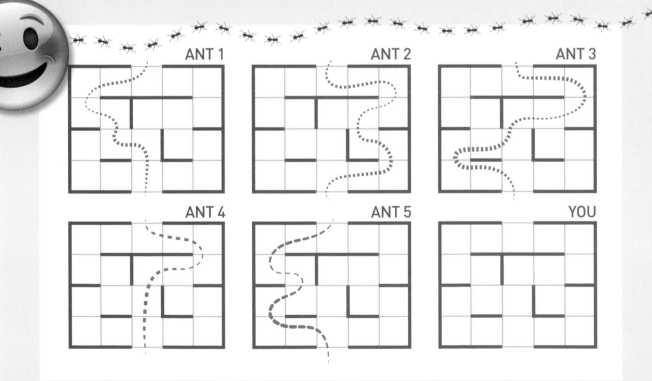

WIGGLE PATTERNS ANSWERS PAGE 154

DID YOU KNOW THAT BEES WIGGLE THEIR BEHINDS TO SPEAK? Just as ants communicate with pheromones, bees quite literally dance to pass on knowledge to their hive-mates! They perform complex sequences of movements to let the other bees know the direction, distance, and quality of sources of pollen. This helps them produce lots of honey, which the bees use as food.

Here are four bee dances and their meanings in terms of the direction to fly to find pollen.

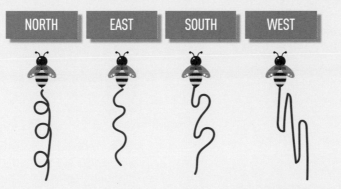

Now take a look at the bee below. What do you think its wiggle dance means? Which of the circled areas on the map do you think it is describing? The hive is in the center of the map, as shown.

PASSING DOWN WISDOM

ELEPHANTS PASS KNOWLEDGE OF THE LOCATIONS OF THE BEST WATERING HOLES AND OTHER IMPORTANT PLACES DOWN TO THEIR YOUNG. We don't know exactly how they do it, but the ability to accurately repeat information to other animals is clearly a critically important skill.

It's also a skill that can make a really fun party game. Gather a group of friends, a bunch of pencils, and a notepad. Sit in a circle, all facing inward. Have someone draw a picture on the first page of the notepad; this could be an elephant, for example, but it can be anything they like. They shouldn't tell anyone else what they're drawing.

Once they've finished their drawing, which ideally would be a simple sketch, they then pass the notepad to the person to their left without showing anyone else what they've drawn. The next person looks at the picture for 10 seconds, and then turns the page and tries to draw it again on the next sheet, without checking back.

This process then repeats, with the next person in each case seeing only the previous person's drawing. Eventually the notepad will make it all the way back around to the start. Compare the final picture with the first one: The differences may be very surprising! If you started with an elephant, you might even end up with a cat, or something completely different, such as a crocodile!

ANIMAL CAMOUFLAGE

ANSWERS PAGE 154

YOU MIGHT THINK THIS FACE WOULD BE PRETTY OBVIOUS IF IT WERE PRINTED SOMEWHERE ELSE ON THIS PAGE AT EXACTLY THE SAME ORIENTATION:

But what if it were on a camouflaged background? Have a look at this picture and see how quickly you can spot the face. It isn't obscured at all, and it looks exactly the same as above:

Did you spot it? Many animals use camouflage patterns to blend into their background; as you can see, it can work very well! You were looking for the face, but if you hadn't known it was there, you might not have spotted it. The same principle applies to animals, such as cheetahs, who are trying to avoid being seen by something that might want to eat them! A cheetah's yellowish brown coat helps it blend in with the tall grasses in its savanna habitat.

AMAZING ANIMAL MEMORY ANSWERS PAGE 154

MANY ANIMALS ARE CAPABLE OF REMARKABLE FEATS OF NAVIGATION. The salmon is one of the most amazing examples: This fish can travel halfway across the world and return to the exact same place in the exact same stream in the exact same country when it is time to lay its eggs. No one knows exactly how they do this, but one possibility is that they take note of certain navigational features as they travel.

Pretend you're a salmon and see if you can use the navigational notes below to travel to the correct location on this map. Start at the "start" marker and then follow the trail to see where you end up. Remember that all the directions are from the point of view of the salmon, so if you are asked to turn right, then do this relative to the direction you are currently traveling!

- ▶ Swim toward the coast.
- ▶ Turn right and follow along the coast.
- ▶ If you see a river, don't enter it; keep swimming along the coast.
- ▶ Pass by a lighthouse on your left and keep swimming.
- ▶ Ignore the first inlet on the left and keep going.
- ▶ Swim into the next inlet you come to.
- ▶ Keep going until the river splits in two.
- ▶ Take the left fork in the river.
- ▶ Swim on, passing under a bridge.
- ▶ Keep going until there is a building on your left-hand side.
- ▶ Congratulations, you've made it!

LAB RATS LEVEL 1 ANSWERS PAGE 154

MICE AND RATS ARE INQUISITIVE CREATURES, and so in laboratory settings they are sometimes placed into mazes to run around and explore. Their behavior is watched by scientists to learn how they react to various conditions. The animal doesn't know where it's going, but by persevering it will eventually find its way through.

Pretend to be a lab rat and solve this maze. Keep track of your progress by using a pencil to mark your route. Enter at the top and see how quickly you can find your way to the exit at the bottom. There's only one solution, so if you reach a dead-end then simply retrace your steps and carry on. You'll need to guess your way through, just like a lab rat would!

START

FINISH

LAB RATS LEVEL 2 ANSWERS PAGE 154

WAS THAT MAZE TOO EASY? Time to take it up a notch! You're obviously smarter than a lab rat, so let's try this tougher maze that now includes bridges. Using the bridges, you can now travel over paths as well as under paths.
Will this maze take you longer to solve, or will you be lucky and run straight through it?

START

FINISH

HEAT SENSING

WE CAN SENSE HEAT AS A GENERAL FEELING OF WARMTH, but some animals with infrared vision can literally see the body heat coming off of other animals. Some snakes, for example, can detect infrared radiation from the warm bodies of their prey. Infrared vision (sometimes called heat vision) also helps snakes avoid animals that want to prey on *them,* since the warm bodies of their predators can be seen even if they are visually well camouflaged.

Infrared vision can even allow animals to see items that are partially obscured, so long as the heat can shine through whatever is blocking the view. Take this photo, for example: Can you see which bush the dog is behind?

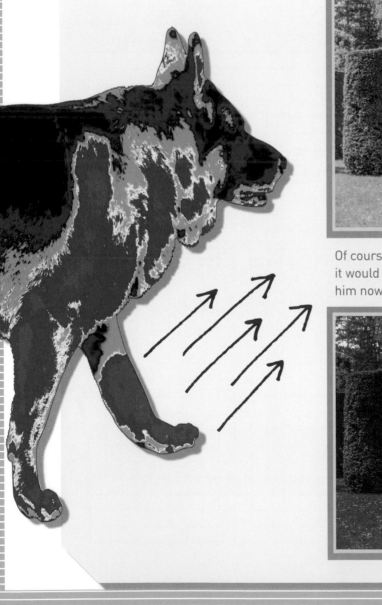

Of course you can't! But check out this image of what it would look like if you had infrared vision. Can you see him now?

THERE HE IS!

CATS' EYES

NOT ONLY DO CATS HAVE AMAZING WHISKERS, they also have the ability to see incredibly well in the dark. Your own eyes have two types of photoreceptors, called rods and cones. The rods don't see in color, but they help provide extra detail as well as peripheral vision—and the ability to see in the dark. Your brain fills in the missing color so you never realize—except when it's dark and everything looks gray—that you aren't seeing in color. The cones are less sensitive, so they don't work very well at night, but they do provide the color you see. Cats have far more rods than cones, relative to you, which means their color vision isn't as good but they can see much better than you when it's dark. Cats also have an extra mirrorlike part in their eye, which helps amplify the light so they can see even better in the dark. This is why their eyes sometimes seem to glow in the dark!

All this nighttime sensitivity means that cats can see more shades of gray than you can. How many shades of gray do you see in the picture below?

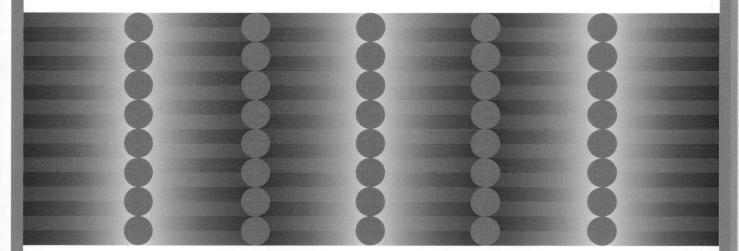

[BEHIND THE BRAIN]

Remarkably, there is only one shade of gray! It looks like there are two shades, but your vision is being influenced by the contrasting colors in the background. Your brain sees the light glow behind two sets of circles and assumes they must be shadowed in front of a bright light. Meanwhile, the others appear to be in front of a dark background, so your clever brain tells you they must be brighter. In this case, the picture has been drawn to deliberately confuse your vision system, but normally this automatic behavior helps you make sense of the world around you!

Grab a scrap piece of paper and cut two small holes in it to line up with two of the adjacent columns of the circles above. Looking through the holes, without the colored background behind, you'll see that the grays are identical.

BOOM!

SPEEDY BEASTS ANSWERS PAGE 155

THE FASTEST SPRINTER ON THE PLANET IS NOT A HUMAN; it's a cheetah. For short distances of up to around 1,500 feet (457 m), cheetahs can run as fast as 75 miles an hour (121 km/h)—that's faster than you'd travel on a highway! A cheetah can also accelerate faster than most sports cars, taking just three seconds to reach 65 miles an hour (105 km/h).

The fastest bird is the peregrine falcon, which can dive downward at more than 240 miles an hour (386 km/h)—almost half the cruising speed of a jet! Meanwhile, the fastest sea animal is probably the black marlin. They can swim as fast as 80 miles an hour (129 km/h)—that's more than twice the speed a cruise ship travels!

In an imaginary race, where every land animal could travel at each of their top speeds for as long as they liked according to the top distances for each animal below, which one would reach the finish line first? Each animal starts at a different point, as shown in the picture below: The cheetah has 15 miles (24 km) to run, the pronghorn antelope has 11 miles (18 km) to run, and the wildebeest has 10 miles (16 km) to run. You can work it out using the formula **time = distance / speed.**

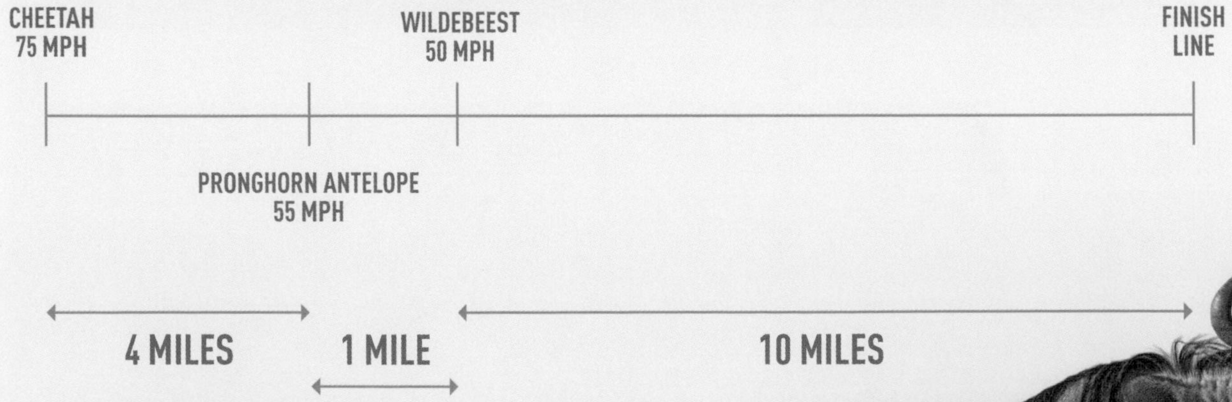

| CHEETAH 75 MPH | | WILDEBEEST 50 MPH | | FINISH LINE |

PRONGHORN ANTELOPE 55 MPH

4 MILES   1 MILE   10 MILES

HERD COUNT ANSWERS PAGE 155

ANIMALS NATURALLY UNDERSTAND THAT THERE IS SAFETY IN NUMBERS AND THAT if faced by various predators, they should move away from the largest group. This means they can glance at a complicated scene and make a good estimate of the relative sizes of groups.

Check out these animal pictures. Can you rank them in order from 1 (most) to 5 (least), based on how many there are of each animal? Give yourself just 10 seconds to answer and then go back and count—did you get it right?

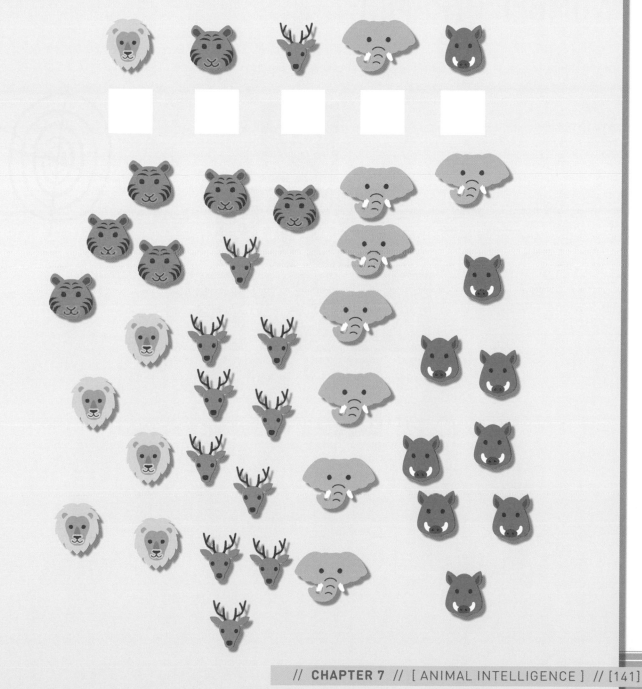

TiME TRiALS

NUMBER PYRAMID ANSWERS PAGE 155

COMPLETE THE NUMBER PYRAMID BY WRITING A NUMBER IN EACH EMPTY SQUARE. Every square in the pyramid must contain a value exactly equal to the total of the two squares immediately beneath it.

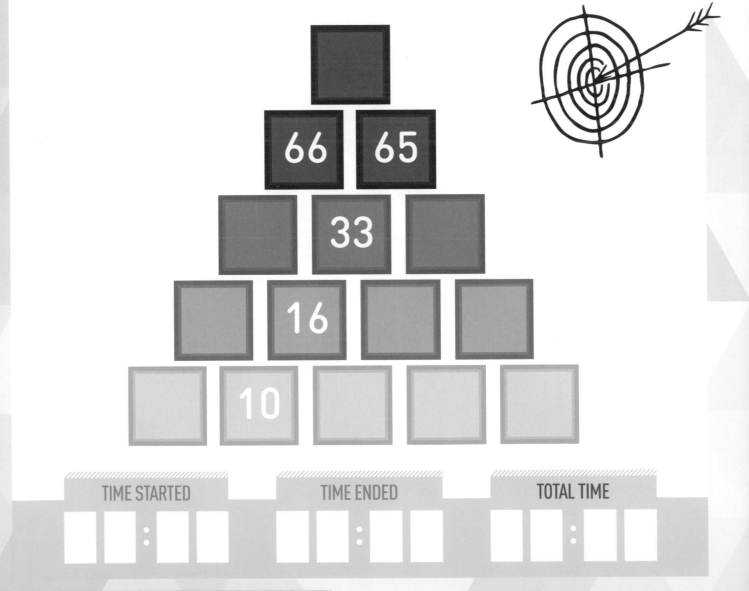

TIME STARTED

TIME ENDED

TOTAL TIME

SIMPLE LOOP ANSWERS PAGE 155

DRAW A SINGLE CLOSED LOOP THAT VISITS EVERY WHITE SQUARE EXACTLY ONCE AND CROSSES NO BLUE SQUARES.
The loop can consist of only horizontal and vertical lines and cannot cross over or touch itself in any way.

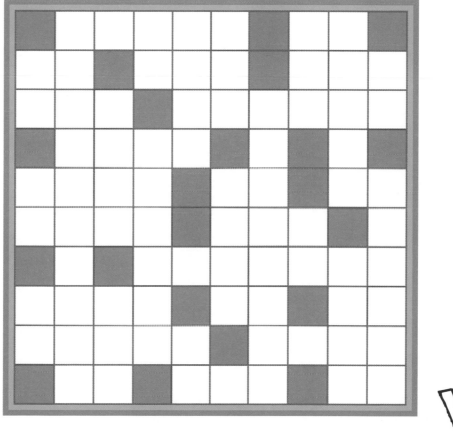

TIME STARTED

☐ ☐ : ☐ ☐

TIME ENDED

☐ ☐ : ☐ ☐

TOTAL TIME

☐ ☐ : ☐ ☐

ANSWERS

CHAPTER TWO

IMAGE COMBINATION PAGE 16, TOP
11 blue hexagons; 9 red circles partially overlapped by blue hexagons; 2 red circles do not overlap with any other shape

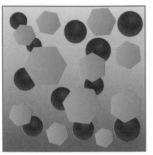

IMAGE STACKING PAGE 16, BOTTOM
A) 3, 4, 2, 1; B) 1, 2, 3, 4

HIDDEN SHAPES PAGE 17, LEFT

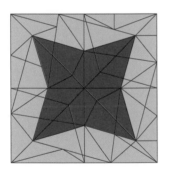

HIDDEN PATTERNS PAGE 17, RIGHT

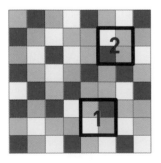

HIDDEN SQUARE PAGE 18, BOTTOM
Up close the pattern is hard to see; but when you step back, the neighboring repeated circles get much closer. The difference seems more "weighty" to the eye and is easier to see.

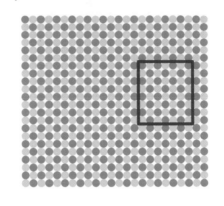

SQUARE DOTS PAGE 19, RIGHT
Because the circles are not placed on the corners of the square, and because the square is tilted, your eye tends to see them as forming a circle. Once that has happened, it's tricky to "re-see" them as a square!

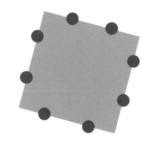

COLOR PATTERNS PAGE 21, BOTTOM

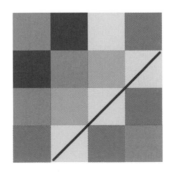

PARTIALLY OBSCURED LINE PAGE 22, TOP
Did you pick one of the lower lines on the right? Nope, it's the second one down. It turns out your brain isn't very good at estimating lengths and projections for anything oriented vertically! This may be because, historically, we've only had to worry about things directly in front of us.

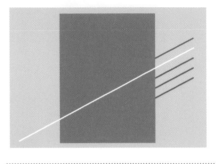

CIRCULAR ARCS PAGE 23, BOTTOM
Did you think that the arcs were all from different-size circles? Take a look at this picture and see if you change your mind: As you can see, all the circles are exactly the same size! Even though the text tells you they are all parts of circles, the visual bit of your brain doesn't know this, and so it makes its own predictions based on just the part of each circle you can actually see. In real life, there aren't hidden circles continuing on from every curve you see, so your brain has no reason to assume this.

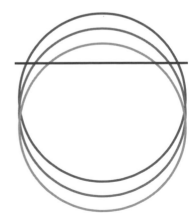

CENTER OF TRIANGLE PAGE 24, LEFT

Surprisingly, the top star is the vertical center. Your brain tends to assume it is the lower of the two stars because it doesn't allow for the height of the narrow extreme top part of the triangle. This is another result of your brain's lack of accuracy when it comes to estimating vertical distances.

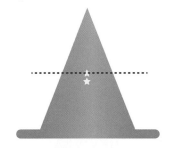

CIRCLE SQUARES PAGE 24, TOP RIGHT

Both orange squares are the exact same size—you can use a ruler to check! Your brain is influenced by the relative sizes of the surrounding objects: Comparatively, the orange square on the left is much bigger than the surrounding blue squares, whereas the orange square on the right is much smaller than its surrounding squares.

MATCHING RECTANGLE PAGE 24, BOTTOM RIGHT

The green rectangle matches the horizontal rectangle at the top of the stack, even though it looks to most people like it matches one of the others. Your brain tends to underestimate vertical heights, compared with its estimation of horizontal widths.

SLIDING CHECKERS PAGE 26

Here's an example of a colored-in image:

NUMBER PYRAMID PAGE 32

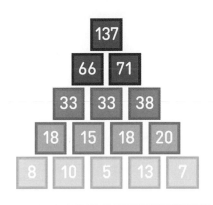

SIMPLE LOOP PAGE 33

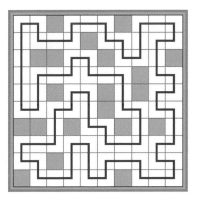

ANSWERS

CHAPTER THREE

WORD PATH PAGE 35
The 12-letter word is HAIRDRESSERS. Other words you might have found include: ads, aid, aide, aides, aids, air, aired, arid, ash, ashes, dash, dashes, die, dire, dress, dresser, dressers, dresses, drier, dries, had, hair, hairdresser, hard, harder, hardier, has, heir, her, herd, herds, hers, ides, ids, ire, raid, raider, raids, rash, rasher, rashes, red, reds, rid, ride, rider, rides, rids, sad, said, sari, shade, shades, shadier, shard, shards, she, shed, sheds, she's

LETTER SOUP PAGE 38, TOP
Green, purple, orange, yellow, brown

BACK-TO-BACK PAGE 38, BOTTOM
Thought, stares, aroma, reader, dozed, yummy, else

MISSING LETTERS PAGE 39, TOP
1. Mom's mom made many yummy summertime meals.
2. Golf balls roll well.
3. Nana's announcing running events now.
4. Gregory's giggling at staggeringly good gags.

DELETED PAIRS PAGE 39, BOTTOM
Cat, tide, loves, clever, dreamer

CRYPTOGRAM PAGE 40, TOP
Congratulations on decoding this secret message. You are a master solver!

BROKEN WORDS PAGE 40, BOTTOM
Monkey, cheetah, giraffe, rhinoceros, chimpanzee, aardvark

ANAGRAM SETS PAGE 41, LEFT
Set 1:
VASTER and AVERTS
PERILS and PLIERS
SWINES and SINEWS
ITSELF and STIFLE

Set 2:
SCENTED and DESCENT
KITCHEN and THICKEN

"STATELY" ANAGRAMS PAGE 41, RIGHT
Colorado, Tennessee, California, Delaware, Washington, Pennsylvania

WORD CHAINS PAGE 42, TOP
TOY → BOY → BUY → BUS
TUG → TAG → TAR → EAR
HERO → HERE → HIRE → TIRE → TIME
SAVE → SALE → MALE → MILE → MILK

WORD PYRAMID PAGE 42, BOTTOM

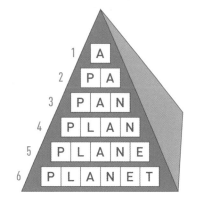

1. A
2. PA
3. PAN
4. PLAN
5. PLANE
6. PLANET

LINK WORDS
PAGE 43, TOP
GOT, to form FORGOT and GOTTEN
BALL, to form BASEBALL and BALL GAME
HILL, to form DOWNHILL and HILLSIDE
WALK, to form CROSSWALK and WALKWAY
DRUM, to form EARDRUM and DRUMSTICKS

PARTIAL TITLES PAGE 43, BOTTOM
Harry Potter and the Sorcerer's Stone
Charlie and the Chocolate Factory
How to Train Your Dragon
Diary of a Wimpy Kid
The Cat in the Hat

CROSSWORD PAGE 44

WORD FIT PAGE 45, TOP

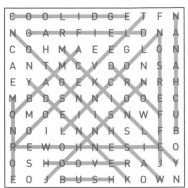

WORD SEARCH PAGE 45, BOTTOM

WORD ANALOGIES PAGE 46, TOP
Four, clean, first, hand, plant

FIND THE SETS PAGE 46, BOTTOM
Red, yellow, green (colors); Mercury, Saturn, Venus (planets); iron, dry, wash (things you do to clothes); Earth, soil, mud (all can refer to soil); orange, apple, banana (fruit); copper, bronze, gold (metals)

ODD WORD OUT PAGE 47, TOP
Lizard—the rest are mammals; White—the others are colors of the rainbow; One—the others are even numbers; Worm—all the other words lack the vowels A, E, I, O, U; Prose—all the others are anagrams of one another

OPPOSITES ATTRACT PAGE 47, BOTTOM
Loud and quiet, soft and hard, easy and difficult, love and hate, come and go, black and white, light and dark, near and far

VOWEL PLAY PAGE 48, LEFT
Wonderful, everyday, tomorrow, pleasant, wildebeest, zucchini

VOWEL TITLES PAGE 48, RIGHT
Beauty and the Beast, The Wizard of Oz, Toy Story, The Incredibles, Frozen, Mary Poppins

ANAGRAM SENTENCES PAGE 49, TOP
Pool, seal, south, treats, diners, reactor

TWO-LETTER SEQUENCES PAGE 49, BOTTOM
Se—numbers: one, two, three, four, five, six, seven; Vi—colors of the rainbow: red, orange, yellow, green, blue, indigo, violet; Ju—months: January, February, March, April, May, June, July; Ur—planets outward from the sun: Mercury, Venus, Earth, Mars, Jupiter, Saturn, Uranus; Se—race positions, also known as "ordinal numbers": first, second, third, fourth, fifth, sixth, seventh

WORDPLAY RIDDLES PAGE 50, LEFT
1) The letter *M*; 2) Incorrectly;
3) Short; 4) The letter *U*; 5) A *B*;
6) In a dictionary

SOUNDALIKES PAGE 50, RIGHT
Faze and phase, eye and I, knight and night, maze and maize, our and hour, reign and rain, scent and cent, whether and weather

HIDDEN PHRASES PAGE 51
Under the weather; the last straw; cut corners (or cutting corners); beat around the bush

LETTER CIRCLES PAGE 52
1) The word using all letters is candies. Other words to find include: aced, acid, acids, ads, aid, aide, aides, aids, and, ands, ascend, aside, cad, cads, caned, cased, dais, dance, dances, dean, deans, den, dens, dice, dices, die, din, dine, dines, dins, disc, end, ends, iced, idea, ideas, ides, ids, sad, said, sand, sedan, send, side, snide.
2) The word using all letters is happier. Other words to find include: ape, are, ear, era, hare, heap, hear, heir, her, hipper, hire, ire, paper, pare, pea, pear, pep, per, pie, pier, pipe, piper, reap, rhea, ripe.
3) The word using all letters is rainbow. Other words to find include: air, bar, barn, baron, boar, born, bra, brain, bran, brawn, brow, brown, iron, nor, oar, orb, rain, ran, raw, rib, roan, rob, robin, row, war, warn, worn.
4) The word using all letters is flowers. Other words to find include: floe, floes, flow, flower, flows, foe, foes, for, fore, fowl, fowls, fro, lore, lose, loser, low, lower, lowers, lows, ore, ores, owe, owes, owl, owls, roe, roes, role, roles, rose, row, rows, sloe, slow, slower, sole, sore, sow, sower, swore, woe, woes, wolf, wolfs, wore, worse.
5) The word using all letters is brilliant. Other words to find include: ail, air, alibi, all, ant, anti, art, bail, bait, ball, ban, bar, barn, bat, bra, brain, bran, brat, lab, lain, lair, liar, lira, nab, nail, rail, rain, ran, rant, rat, tab, tail, tall, tan, tar, tibia, trail, train, trial, tribal.

6) The word using all letters is transport. Other words to find include: apron, aprons, arson, atop, nor, not, oar, oars, opt, opts, parrot, parrots, parson, pastor, patron, patrons, port, ports, post, pot, pots, pro, pros, roan, roans, roar, roars, roast, rot, rots, snort, soap, soar, son, sonar, sop, sort, sporran, sport, spot, stoat, stop, strop, taro, taros, toast, ton, tons, top, tops, tor, torn, tors, tot, tots, trot, trots.

NUMBER PYRAMID PAGE 54
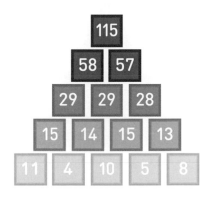

SIMPLE LOOP PAGE 55
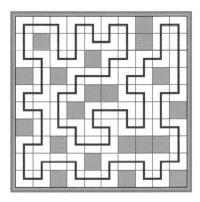

ANSWERS

CHAPTER FOUR

COIN CONUNDRUM PAGE 57
Did you figure it out? The solution is a bit sneaky because it requires you to place one coin on top of the others, like this:

CUBE NETS PAGE 60, TOP

ODD CUBE OUT PAGE 60, BOTTOM
Cube net 2 is different. The black arrow points in the opposite direction compared to the other cubes.

PYRAMID NETS PAGE 61, LEFT

ODD PYRAMID OUT PAGE 61, RIGHT
Pyramid B. The shape on the right-hand-side face should be the brown triangle.

SHAPE LINK PAGE 62, LEFT

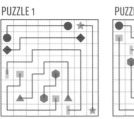

PUZZLE 1   PUZZLE 2

SHAPE DIVISION PAGE 62, RIGHT

PUZZLE 1   PUZZLE 2

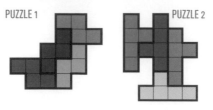

AREA DIVISION PAGE 63

PUZZLE 1   PUZZLE 2

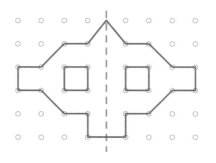

DRAW REFLECTIONS PAGE 64, TOP

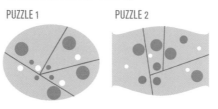

IDENTITY REFLECTED PAGE 64, BOTTOM
1C, 2B, 3A

IDENTITY ROTATED PAGE 65, TOP
1B, 2C, 3B

WHEEL ROTATION PAGE 65, BOTTOM
B

JIGSAW PIECES PAGE 66, TOP
A, B, and C

KEY IMPRESSIONS PAGE 66, BOTTOM
B

3-D CUBE COUNTING PAGE 68, LEFT
Top: 23 cubes, made up as follows: top level = 4 cubes, middle level = 8 cubes, bottom level = 11 cubes
Bottom: 15 cubes, made up as follows: top level = 2 cubes, middle level = 4 cubes, bottom level = 9 cubes

SHAPE COUNTING PAGE 68, RIGHT
There are 31 rectangles and squares in total. The easiest way to count is to consider each intersection in the picture in turn. Imagine that it is a corner of a rectangle/square, and see how many you can make using that point as the top-left corner. Make a note on the picture, and repeat for all corners. Then add up your totals.

SLIDING LETTERS PAGE 69, TOP

SHADOW MATCH PAGE 69, BOTTOM
C

MAP ROTATION PAGE 70
Option 3

MAP READING PAGE 71, LEFT
Here is how you could have described the routes:
Hospital: Go straight over the first two intersections you come to, and then turn right at the next intersection. Continue along the road until you pass a turn off to your left. The hospital is just a bit farther along, on your left.
Gas station: Go straight, crossing over two intersections and then turning left at the third one. Continue along this road and take the next right. The gas station is halfway along the road on your right.

MAZE SOLVING PAGE 71, RIGHT
Option 2

JOIN THE DOTS PAGE 72, TOP
This puzzle is tricky because you need to draw the path outside the boundary of the square formed by the nine dots. Instinctively, it's tempting to stay within that imaginary boundary.

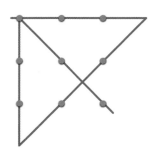

BOX THE DOTS PAGE 72, BOTTOM
The solution to this puzzle also requires some clever thinking. The secret is to rotate one of the squares 45 degrees, like this:

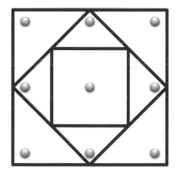

DOT TO DOT PAGE 73
It's a "+" sign:

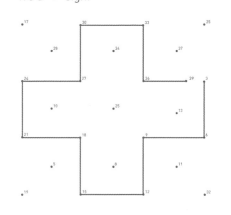

PLUGS AND SOCKETS PAGE 74, TOP

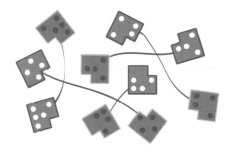

3-D VIEWS PAGE 74, BOTTOM

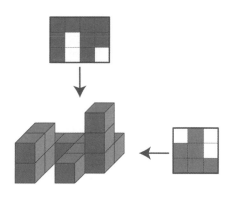

3-D ROTATIONS PAGE 75
Arrangement E

NUMBER PYRAMID PAGE 76

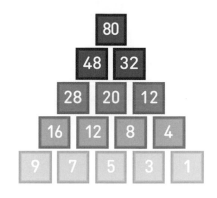

SIMPLE LOOP PAGE 77

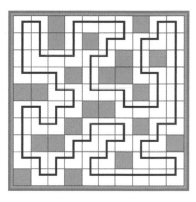

ANSWERS

CHAPTER FIVE

LIQUID PROBLEM PAGE 79
1) Pour C into B to get 0 pints in A, 5 pints in B, and 2 pints in C.
2) Then pour B into A to get 2 pints in A, 3 pints in B, and 2 pints in C.
3) Next pour A into C to get 0 pints in A, 3 pints in B, and 4 pints in C.
4) Then pour B into A. At this point you have totals of 2 pints in A, 1 pint in B, and 4 pints in C.
5) Finally, pour A into C—and you're done! You now have 0 pints in A, 1 pint in B, and 6 pints in C.

IT'S LOGICAL PAGE 82, TOP

Brother	Age	Hobby
Andy	13 years	Swimming
Bart	11 years	Singing
Cliff	9 years	Reading

SAND TIME CHALLENGE PAGE 82, BOTTOM
Turn over both timers at the same time. Once the four-minute one finishes, turn it straight back over so the sand starts flowing again. Then, when the five-minute one finishes, turn the four-minute one over again even though it hasn't finished. One minute of sand will have flowed through it, so it will take it another minute for it to flow back through again. Therefore, when the four-minute one finishes again, exactly six minutes will have passed!

BALANCE PAGE 83, TOP
The circle is lightest, and the triangle is heaviest. You can work this out because on the left balance, the two circles weigh the same on each side so can be ignored; therefore, the triangle is heavier than the square. On the right balance, the square on the left side weighs the same as one of the squares on the right side, so you can see that the single square weighs more than the circle. So the triangle weighs more than the square, which in turn weighs more than the circle.

TOWER OF HANOI PAGE 83, BOTTOM
Move 1 from A to C. Move 2 from A to B. Move 1 from C to B. Move 3 from A to C. Move 1 from B to A. Move 2 from B to C. Move 1 from A to C. Finished!

VISUAL SEQUENCES PAGE 84
Option A—At each step, the number of sides on the shape increases by 1.
Option C—At each step, the spiral rotates 90 degrees around the outside of the shape, and the star moves clockwise to the next corner.

TIME CLASH PAGE 85, TOP
The upper clock face displays 8:30 and 10:34, while the lower clock face displays 5:10 and 7:22.

MATCHSTICKS PAGE 85, BOTTOM

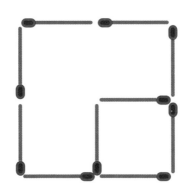

NUMBER SEQUENCES PAGE 86, TOP
A) 21—multiples of 3
B) 9—subtract 4 at each step
C) 64—multiply by 2 at each step
D) 1—divide by 3 at each step
E) 31—prime numbers in increasing order

NUMBER DARTS PAGE 86, BOTTOM
19 = 2 + 5 + 12
26 = 11 + 7 + 8
33 = 11 + 7 + 15

NUMBER ANAGRAMS PAGE 87, TOP
(1 + 3) × 4 + 6 = 22
6 × (1 + 3 + 4) = 48

NUMBER BUDDIES PAGE 87, BOTTOM
×2: 3 & 6, 12 & 24, 17 & 34, 5 & 10, 20 & 40
×5: 2 & 10, 3 & 15, 50 & 250, 4 & 20, 5 & 25
÷3: 9 & 3, 81 & 27, 6 & 2, 54 & 18, 12 & 4

SORTING SUMS PAGE 88, TOP
B A C E D

NUMBER MAZE PAGE 88, BOTTOM

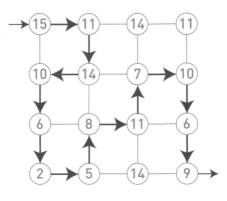

BRAIN CHAINS PAGE 89, TOP

12	13	6	48	36	RESULT 43
15	5	10	22	13	RESULT 28
11	2	24	6	25	RESULT 5

RECTANGULAR DIVISION PAGE 89, BOTTOM

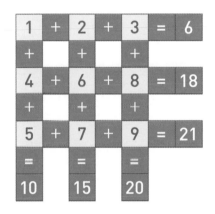

ARITHMETIC SQUARE PAGE 90, TOP

1	+	2	+	3	=	6
+		+		+		
4	+	6	+	8	=	18
+		+		+		
5	+	7	+	9	=	21
=		=		=		
10		15		20		

NUMBER EQUATIONS PAGE 90, BOTTOM

🍎 = 2   🍊 = 5

🍐 = 3   🍋 = 1   🫐 = 4

COIN PUZZLES PAGE 91, LEFT

7 coins: 25¢ + 25¢ + 25¢ + 10¢ + 1¢ + 1¢ + 1¢

4 coins: my change is 37¢, made up of 25¢ + 10¢ + 1¢ + 1¢

FLOATING NUMBERS PAGE 91, RIGHT

20 = 4 + 6 + 10
30 = 7 + 11 + 12
35 = 6 + 7 + 10 + 12

FENCES PAGE 92, LEFT

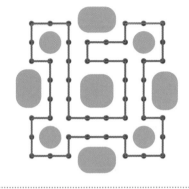

LATIN SQUARE PAGE 92, RIGHT

4	6	1	3	5	2
3	1	5	4	2	6
1	2	6	5	3	4
5	4	3	2	6	1
6	3	2	1	4	5
2	5	4	6	1	3

TOUCHY NUMBERS PAGE 93, LEFT

4	5	2	1	6	3
2	1	6	3	5	4
6	3	5	4	1	2
5	4	1	2	3	6
1	2	3	6	4	5
3	6	4	5	2	1

INEQUALITY PUZZLE PAGE 93, RIGHT

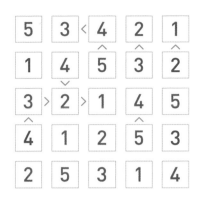

5	3	4	2	1
1	4	5	3	2
3	2	1	4	5
4	1	2	5	3
2	5	3	1	4

ONES AND ZEROS PAGE 94, TOP

1	0	0	1	1	0
0	1	0	0	1	1
0	0	1	1	0	1
1	1	0	0	1	0
0	1	1	0	0	1
1	0	1	1	0	0

PATHFINDER PAGE 94, BOTTOM

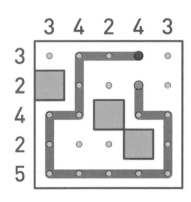

ANSWERS

NUMBER JOURNEY PAGE 95, LEFT

1	4	5	34	35	36
2	3	6	33	30	29
9	8	7	32	31	28
10	11	12	13	26	27
17	16	15	14	25	24
18	19	20	21	22	23

KING'S JOURNEY PAGE 95, RIGHT

22	21	20	17	16
23	24	18	19	15
25	5	6	12	14
4	1	7	11	13
2	3	8	9	10

MINIATURE SUDOKU PAGE 96, LEFT

1	2	3	4
4	3	2	1
2	1	4	3
3	4	1	2

2	1	4	3
3	4	1	2
4	3	2	1
1	2	3	4

4	3	2	1
2	1	4	3
1	4	3	2
3	2	1	4

1	4	3	2
3	2	4	1
4	1	2	3
2	3	1	4

JIGSAW LETTERS PAGE 96, RIGHT

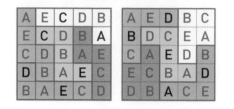

3-D SUDOKU PAGE 97, TOP

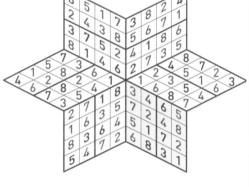

SAMURAI SUDOKU PAGE 97, BOTTOM

3	2	5	6	1	4
5	4	1	3	2	6
1	6	2	4	5	3
6	5	4	1	3	2	5	6
2	3	6	5	4	1	2	3
4	1	3	2	6	5	1	4

5	4	1	3	6	2	4	5
2	6	5	4	3	1	2	6
1	3	2	6	4	5	3	1
6	1	4	5	3
4	5	1	3	6	2
3	2	5	6	1	4

NUMBER PYRAMID PAGE 98

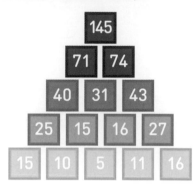

SIMPLE LOOP PAGE 99

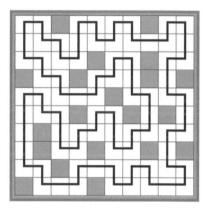

CHAPTER SIX

JUMBLED WORDS PAGE 104, TOP
THIS EXAMPLE IS QUITE DIFFICULT TO READ.

INVERTED WORDS PAGE 104, BOTTOM
DIMES

SHADOW WORDS PAGE 105, TOP
CLIMATE

OVERLAID WORDS PAGE 105, BOTTOM
CLEVER
BRAINS

VISUAL CONFUSION PAGE 106, BOTTOM

ROUNDING AND ESTIMATION
PAGE 109, TOP
The precise answer is $71.98, but our estimation method should have given you a total of $71. Not bad!

IMAGE MEMORY PAGE 110

MISSING WORDS PAGE 112, TOP
Unique, Dreamer, Reference

SHAPE ORDER PAGE 112, BOTTOM
6, 10, 8, 3, 2, 9, 5, 1, 4, 7

WORD SEARCH MEMORY PAGE 113

NO FOUR IN A ROW PAGE 114, LEFT

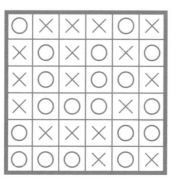

MINDSWEEPER PAGE 114, RIGHT

TANGRAMS PAGE 117, RIGHT

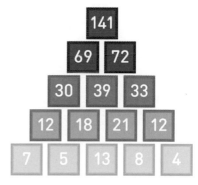

NUMBER PYRAMID PAGE 120

SIMPLE LOOP PAGE 121

ANSWERS

CHAPTER SEVEN

BLACK-AND-WHITE VERSUS COLOR VISION PAGE 126

The stream on the left of the image is particularly hard to identify in black and white, but also the perspective on the fencing near the center is also very confusing without any color cues.

CELLULAR VISION PAGE 127

The picture is of the White House, in Washington, D.C.

HUMMINGBIRD HOVER POWER
PAGE 129, RIGHT

If a human needed to consume as many calories as a hummingbird, they'd need to eat 2,000 × 75 = 150,000 calories per day!

SQUIRREL SKILLS PAGE 130

Platform B

SUPER SENSE OF SMELL PAGE 131

Exit D

ANT PHEROMONES PAGE 132

2	2	5	3	3
2	2	2	3	3
2	3	3	1	1
2	2	5	1	1

WIGGLE PATTERNS PAGE 133

The bee is wiggling "north" followed by "west," so it is directing the other bees toward the hills, circled at the top-left of the map. These are northwest of the hive, as can be seen from the compass included at the top-right of the map.

ANIMAL CAMOUFLAGE PAGE 134, RIGHT

AMAZING ANIMAL MEMORY PAGE 135

The destination is marked with a red circle.

LAB RATS LEVEL 1 PAGE 136

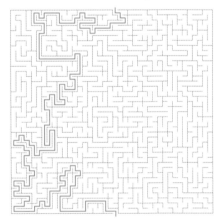

LAB RATS LEVEL 2 PAGE 137

SPEEDY BEASTS PAGE 140

It would be a draw! All three would finish at the same time.
Cheetah: 15 miles (24 km) / 75 mph (121 km/h) = 0.2 hours (that is, 12 minutes)
Pronghorn antelope: 11 miles (18 km) / 55 mph (89 km/h) = 0.2 hours
Wildebeest: 10 miles (16 km) / 50 mph (81 km/h) = 0.2 hours

HERD COUNT PAGE 141

| 5 | 4 | 1 | 3 | 2 |

NUMBER PYRAMID PAGE 142

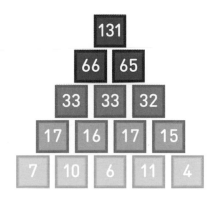

SIMPLE LOOP PAGE 143

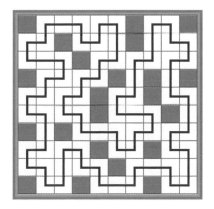

INDEX

Boldface indicates illustrations.

A

Accidents and injuries 11, 36–37
Animal intelligence 122–143
  bees 124–125, **125**, 133, **133**
  cephalopods 124, **124**
  communication 34, 124–125, 133
  crows 125, **125**
  puzzles & games 123, 126–143, 154–155
Answers to puzzles & games 144–155
Ant pheromones 132
Artificial intelligence voices 81

B

Bees 124–125, **125**, 133, **133**
Birds of prey 129, 140
Blind people 28
Blind spot 15, 23
Brain
  injuries 11, 36–37
  introduction 6–7
  lobes 8, **8–9**
  nerve network 8
  right brain and left brain 10
  tools for studying 10–11, **11**
Brain mysteries 100–121
  dreams 103
  language of the brain 102

memory storage 102
puzzles & games 101, 104–121, 153
sleep 102
Broca, Paul 36
Broca's area 36, **36**

C

Cats 139, **139**
Cephalopods 124, **124**
Cerebrum 8
Cheetahs 140, **140**
Color vision 13, 20, 126
Communication see Animal intelligence; Words and language
Complementary colors 20
Computed tomography (CT) 10, **11**
Computers, robot takeover? 80–81, **81**
Corpus callosum 10
Creative and emotional tasks 10
Crows 125, **125**
CT (computed tomography) 10, **11**
Cuttlefish 124, **124**

D

Daydreaming 80
Deaf people 37
Decision making 8
Dogs 131, **131**
Dreams 103

E

EEG (electroencephalography) 10
Ehrenstein illusion 22
Electricity 8, 10, 14, 102
Elephants 134, **134**

F

Flies 127, **127**
FMRI (functional MRI) 11, **11**, 80
Freud, Sigmund 102
Frontal lobe 8, **9**, 59, 78
Functional MRI (fMRI) 11, **11**, 80

G

Gage, Phineas 11
Games see Puzzles & games

H

Harlow, John 11
Hearing, sense of 8, 29, 36, **36**
Hering illusion 19
Hippocampus 58, **58**
Honeybees 124–125, **125**, 133, **133**
Hummingbirds 129, **129**

I

Imaging the brain 10–11, **11**
Injuries and accidents 11, 36–37
Insight 80

J

Jennings, Ken 80, **81**
Jeopardy! (TV show) 80, **81**

L

Language *see* Words and
   language
Left brain 10, 36–37
Lobes 8
Logic and rational thinking 10,
   80–81
Long-term memory 102

M

Magnetic resonance imaging
   (MRI) 11, **11**, 59, 88
Magnetoencephalography (MEG)
   11
Map reading 70
Mars rovers 80–81, **81**
Math 10, 80, 88
MEG (magnetoencephalography)
   11
Memory 8, 102, 135
Mental mapmaking 58–59
Mind map 8
MRI (magnetic resonance
   imaging) 11, **11**, 59, 88
Music 37
Mysteries *see* Brain mysteries

N

Neurons (nerve cells) 8, 9, **11**, 58,
   102
Nociception 14

O

Occipital lobe 8, **9**
Octopus 124
Optic nerve 14, 15, 23
Optical illusions 18, 19

P

Pain, sense of 14
Parietal lobe 8, **9**, 58, **58**
Patterns 17, 18, 48
Peregrine falcons 140
Personality 11
PET/CT scan **11**
Pheromones 132
Pigeons 128, **128**
Problem solving 78–99
   frontal lobe control 8, 78
   insight 80
   logical learning 80–81
   math steps 88
   puzzles & games 79, 82–99,
      150–152
   robot takeover? 80–81
Proprioception 14
Puzzles & games
   animal intelligence 123, 126–
      143, 154–155

answers 144–155
brain mysteries 101, 104–121,
   153
problem solving 79, 82–99,
   150–152
senses 13, 16–33, 144–145
spatial smarts 57, 60–77,
   148–149
time trials 32–33, 54–55, 76–77,
   98–99, 120–121, 142–143
words and language 35, 38–55,
   146–147

R

Reasoning 8
REM (rapid eye movement) sleep
   103
Right brain 10, 36–37
Robot takeover? 80–81
Rods and cones 139

S

Salmon 135
Senses 12–33
   hidden senses 14
   parietal lobe processing 8
   puzzles & games 13, 16–33,
      144–145
   see also Hearing; Smell; Taste;
      Touch; Vision
Short-term memory 102
Sign language 37

INDEX

Sleep 102, 103
Smell, sense of 8, 28, 131, 132
Snakes 138
Sound *see* Hearing, sense of
Spatial smarts 56–77
    brain building 59
    mental mapmaking 58–59
    puzzles & games 57, 60–77,
      148–149
    visual thinking 58–59
Speech production 36
Squirrels 130, **130**

T

Taste, sense of 8, 28, 29
Temperature, sense of 8, 138, **138**
Temporal lobe 8, **9**
Temporal perception 14, 30
Tetris 59, **59**
Thoughts, daily number of 15
3-D vision 14–15
Time, sense of 14, 30
Time trials 32–33, 54–55, 76–77,
    98–99, 120–121, 142–143
Touch, sense of 28

U

Unconscious mind 102

V

Vanishing colors 13, **13**

Vision 14–15
    animals 126–129, 138, **138,**
      139, **139**
    blind spot 15, 23
    how it works 14, **14**
    limits 14–15
    occipital lobe processing 8
    puzzles & games 13, 16–27
    3-D vision 14–15
    tricking the mind 15
Visual thinking *see* Spatial smarts

W

Water, as percentage of brain 11
Watson (computer) 80–81, **81**
Wernicke, Carl 36
Wernicke's area 36, **36**
Words and language 34–55
    animal communication 34,
      124–125
    how it works **36,** 36–37
    language of the brain 102
    math as universal language 80
    puzzle & games 35, 38–55,
      146–147
    temporal lobe processing 8

PHOTO CREDITS

SS = SHUTTERSTOCK
ALL PUZZLE ART BY DR. GARETH MOORE UNLESS NOTED BELOW:
COVER (MAZE), KCHUNGTW/GETTY IMAGES; (BOY), NALUWAN/SS; (PEN), TALIZORA/SS; (ILLUSION), YOUTHS/DREAMSTIME; (MATH), TALIZORA/SS; (ROBOT), THOMASVOGE/GETTY IMAGES; (HAND), TALIZORA/SS; (BRAIN), JEONG SUH/BRYAN CHRISTIE DESIGN; (LIGHTBULB), PIO3/SS; (DINO), LONGLAIR/DREAMSTIME; (BOOK), TALIZORA/SS; (EMOJI), OBER-ART/SS; (SMILIES), TALIZORA/SS; (BUBBLE), TALIZORA/SS; (ARROW), JOHAVEL/SS; BACK COVER (MAZE), KCHUNGTW/GETTY IMAGES; (EMOJI), OBER-ART/SS; (STICKY), MARTINA VACULIKOVA/SS; (OWL), CYNTHIA KIDWELL/SS; (BUBBLE), TALIZORA/SS; 2 (LO CTR), SEVENKE/SS; 2 (LIGHTBULB), PIO3/SS; 2 PEN, TALIZORA/SS; 3, KCHUNGTW/GETTY IMAGES; 4-5 (HEXAGON BACKGROUND THROUGHOUT), YANIE; 4 (DINO), LONGLAIR/DREAMSTIME; 4 (BOOK), TALIZORA/SS; 4 (LO CTR), THOMASVOGE/GETTY IMAGES; 5 (STICKY PAPER THROUGHOUT), MARTINA VACULIKOVA/SS; 5 (BOY), NALUWAN/SS; 5 (ILLUSION), YOUTHS/DREAMSTIME; 5 (LIGHTBULB), PIO3/SS; 5 (BUBBLE), TALIZORA/SS; 6-7 (BRAIN BACKGROUND THROUGHOUT), GRANDEDUC/SS; 9, JEONG SUH/BRYAN CHRISTIE DESIGN; 10 (LO), ERANICLE/SS; 11 (LE), STEGERPHOTO/GETTY IMAGES; 11 (UP RT), BARANOZDEMIR/GETTY IMAGES; 11 (CTR RT), SARANS/SS; 12-13 (BACKGROUND), GRANDEDUC/SS; 13 (ARROW), JOHAVEL/SS; 14, SPENCER SUTTON/SCIENCE SOURCE; 15 (UP LE), VITSTUDIO/SS; 15 (UP RT), POPCORNER/SS; 15 (CTR LE), BILLION PHOTOS/SS; 15 (CTR RT), YONGNIAN GUI/DREAMSTIME; 15 (LIGHTBULB), PIO3/SS; 15 (LO RT), REDPIXEL.PL/SS; 16 (ARROW), PIO3/SS; 17 (BUBBLE), PIO3/SS; 17 (ARROW), JOHAVEL/SS; 18 (SCRIBBLE), PIO3/SS; 19 (ARROW), JOHAVEL/SS; 20 (BUBBLE), TALIZORA/SS; 21 (ARROW), JOHAVEL/SS; 22 (BUBBLE), TALIZORA/SS; 22 (EMOJIS THROUGHOUT), OBER-ART/SS; 23 (EYE), TALIZORA/SS; 23 (QUESTIONS), PIO3/SS; 24 (GEARS), TALIZORA/SS; 24 (RULER), TALIZORA/SS; 25 (BUBBLE), TALIZORA/SS; 26 (PEN), TALIZORA/SS; 27 (BUBBLE), TALIZORA/SS; 28 (COINS), STILLFX/SS; 28 (UP RT), 5 SECOND STUDIO/SS; 28 (CTR LE), ANTONIO GUILLEM/SS; 28 (BUBBLE), PIO3/SS; 29 (UP), KURHAN/SS; 29 (APPLES), NEBOJSA BABIC/DREAMSTIME; 29 (SPOON), ONAIR/SS; 29 (EMOJI), OBER-ART/SS; 30 (UP RT), ALEX STAROSELTSEV/SS; 30 (TIME), TALIZORA/SS; 31 (UP RT), KAMENETSKIY KONSTANTIN/SS; 31 (LO LE), SEVDALINA ANGELOVA/SS; 31 (BUBBLES), PIO3/SS; 32-33 (TRIANGLE BACKGROUND THROUGHOUT), MELAMORY/SS; 32 (CALCULATOR), TALIZORA/SS; 33 (EMOJI), OBER-ART/SS; 33 (ARROW), TALIZORA/SS; 34 (GRAPHICS), TALIZORA/SS; 35 (ARROW), JOHAVEL/SS; 36, JEONG SUH/BRYAN CHRISTIE DESIGN; 37 (UP LE), JOSEPH/SS; 37 (UP RT), LOVE LOVE/SS; 37 (CTR LE), EUGENE LU/SS; 37 (CTR RT), PAFFY/SS; 37 (LIGHTBULB), PIO3/SS; 37 (LO), SPLINE_X/SS; 38 (ARROW), JOHAVEL/SS; 38 (SPOON), MODUZA DESIGN; 39 (QUESTION MARK), PIO3/SS; 39 (LO RT), PZAXE/SS; 40 (SCRIBBLE), PIO3/SS; 40 (LO), ERIC ISSELEE/SS; 41 (UP RT), OHMEGA1982/SS; 41 (ARROWS), PIO3/SS; 42, (CHAIN), MODUZA DESIGN; 43 (LO RT), URFIN/SS; 44 (BUBBLE), TALIZORA/SS; 45 (LO), JOSEPH SOHM/SS; 46-47 (BACKGROUND), KEVIN KEY/SS; 46 (UP), AGUITERS/SS; 46 (CIRCLES), PIO3/SS; 47 (UP RT), REPTILES4ALL/SS; 47 (BUBBLE), TALIZORA/SS; 48 (LO), CHONES/SS; 49 (ARROWS), PIO3/SS; 49 (NUMBER), SCHNEEEULE/SS; 50 (UP RT), VLADIMIR GJORGIEV/SS; 52 (WATCH), COURGARSAN/SS; 52 (WATCH ICONS), GN ILLUSTRATOR/SS; 53 (PEN), TALIZORA/SS; 53 (ARROWS), PIO3/SS; 53 (LO LE), KARAMYSH/SS; 53 (LO RT), JULES_KITANO/SS; 54 (ARROW), JOHAVEL/SS; 55 (SPIRAL), TALIZORA/SS; 56 (GRAPHICS), PIO3/SS; 57 (UP), PHOTKA/SS; 57 (BUBBLE), PIO3/SS; 57 (CTR), STILLFX/SS; 58 (UP), PIO3/SS; 58 (LO), JEONG SUH/BRYAN CHRISTIE DESIGN; 59 (UP LE), KOSMOS111/SS; 59 (UP RT), AMY JOHANSSON/SS; 59 (CTR LE), SVISIO/GETTY IMAGES; 59 (CTR RT), KLEBER CORDEIRO/SS; 59 (LIGHTBULB), PIO3/SS; 59 (LO), BOBNEVV/SS; 60 (SPIRAL), TALIZORA/SS; 61 (PUNCTUATION), TALIZORA/SS; 63 (UP RT), PHOTKA/SS; 64 (ARROWS), PIO3/SS; 65 (SPIRAL), PIO3/SS; 66 (UP RT), DOMNITSKY/SS; 66 (CTR LE), MODUZA DESIGN; 66 (LO RT), SUNS07BUTTERFLY/SS; 67 (BUBBLE), TALIZORA/SS; 68 (ARROWS), PIO3/SS; 68 (MATH), TALIZORA/SS; 69 (SUN), MODUZA DESIGN; 70 (COMPASS), TALIZORA/SS; 70 (MAP), ART ALEX/SS; 70 (GRAPHICS), TALIZORA/SS; 72 (PENCIL), TALIZORA/SS; 72 (ARROW), TALIZORA/SS; 73 (HAND), TALIZORA/SS; 75 (GEARS), TALIZORA/SS; 76 (CLOCK), PIO3/SS; 77 (ARROWS), TALIZORA/SS; 78 (PUZZLE), TALIZORA/SS; 78 (ARROW), JOHAVEL/SS; 78 (PIE CHART), PIO3/SS; 79 (GRAPHICS), TALIZORA/SS; 80-81 (EQUATIONS), ARTMARI/SS; 81 (UP LE), MENNOVANDIJK/GETTY IMAGES; 81 (UP RT), NASA/JPL-CALTECH; 81 (CTR LE), PIXDELUXE/GETTY IMAGES; 81 (CTR RT), SETH WENIG/AP/REX/SS; 81 (LIGHTBULB), PIO3/SS; 82 (UP RT), PIO3/SS; 83 (BOOKS), PROKRIDA/SS; 84 (CHECK BOXES), PIO3/SS; 85 (CLOCK), TALIZORA/SS; 85 (LO LE), BUTTERFLY HUNTER/SS; 86 (BUBBLE), TALIZORA/SS; 87 (HEARTS), TALIZORA/SS; 88 (UP RT), VITALY KOROVIN/SS; 88 (SPIRAL), TALIZORA/SS; 90 (LO RT), ROMAN SAMOKHIN/SS; 91 (UP RT), VIRINAFLORA/SS; 91 (LO LE), CAROLYN FRANKS/SS; 92-93 (BACKGROUND), JOHANNES KORNELIUS/SS; 92 (CIRCLE), TALIZORA/SS; 93 (UP), VECTOR-RGB/SS; 94 (BACKGROUND), MSSA/SS; 94 (LO RT), TALIZORA/SS; 95 (UP RT), IVAN PONOMAREV/SS; 96 (UP RT), RINELLE/SS; 96 (LO LE), TALIZORA/SS; 97 (CTR LE), MEGA PIXEL/SS; 97 (LO RT), TALIZORA/SS; 98 (LO LE), JOHAVEL/SS; 99 (UP RT), TALIZORA/SS; 100 (SKETCHES), MODUZA DESIGN; 101 (SWIRL), TALIZORA/SS; 103 (UP LE), ALONES/SS; 103 (UP RT), MRIMAN/SS; 103 (CTR RT), CANETTISTOCK/DREAMSTIME; 103 (LIGHTBULB), PIO3/SS; 103 (LO), ALLISON HERROLD/SS; 104 (ARROWS), JOHAVEL/SS; 105 (UP RT), TALIZORA/SS; 105 (CTR LE), PIO3/SS; 106 (GRAPHICS), TALIZORA/SS; 106 (UP), FILIP WARULIK/SS; 106 (LO), TOP PHOTO ENGINEER/SS; 107 (ARROWS), TALIZORA/SS; 107 (UP LE), DG STOCK/SS; 107 (UP RT), STEVE WELSH/ALAMY STOCK PHOTO; 107 (LO LE), DARRYL GILL/ALAMY STOCK PHOTO; 107 (LO RT), GOGADICTA/GETTY IMAGES; 108 (PENCIL), TALIZORA/SS; 109 (UP RT), FOTOCRISIS/SS; 109 (PUSHPIN), TALIZORA/SS; 110 (BUBBLE), TALIZORA/SS; 111 (UP CTR), RATIKOVA/SS; 111 (UP RT), TIM UR/SS; 111 (CTR), KELLIS/SS; 111 (LO), HURST PHOTO/SS; 112 (UP LE), MIRASWONDERLAND/SS; 112 (TARGET), TALIZORA/SS; 113 (UP CTR), MAYAKOVA/SS; 113 (UP RT), INGVALD KALDHUSSATER/SS; 113 (LO RT), IADAMS/SS; 114 (HAND), TALIZORA/SS; 114 (LO LE), ALEKS MELNIK/SS; 115 (UP RT), KARPENKO_ILIA/SS; 115 (LO RT), PRASIT SUKKUL/SS; 116 (ARROWS), TALIZORA/SS; 116 (CTR), OPICOBELLO/SS; 116 (BUBBLE), TALIZORA/SS; 116 (LO), MODUZA DESIGN; 116 (LO RT), IRINA ZHOLUDEVA/SS; 117 (PEN), PIO3/SS; 118 (LO LE), MANEKINA SERAFIMA/SS; 118 (PUZZLE), TALIZORA/SS; 119 (UP RT), CHAMILLE WHITE/SS; 119 (CTR LE), OLEGGANKO/SS; 120 (ARROWS), TALIZORA/SS; 122 (SKETCHES), MODUZA DESIGN; 124, DAVID LITMAN/SS; 125 (LE), SIMUN ASCIC/SS; 125 (RT), CRISTIAN GUSA/SS; 125 (LIGHTBULB), PIO3/SS; 126 (BUBBLE), TALIZORA/SS; 126 (LE), TAKAHASHI_4/SS; 126 (RT), CYNTHIA KIDWELL/SS; 127 (UP), VITALIJ TERESCSUK/SS; 127 (CTR), TURTIX/SS; 127 (LO), NATALIIA K/SS; 128-129 (BACKGROUND), KZWW/SS; 128 (UP), PHOTOMASTER/SS; 128 (CTR), JOHNATHAN AMPERSAND ESPER/GETTY IMAGES; 128 (LO LE), VLADIMIR GRAMAGIN/SS; 128 (LO RT), FRANCESCO FERRARINI/SS; 128 (ARROWS), JOHAVEL/SS; 129 (UP RT), VISUAL GENERATION/SS; 129 (CTR LE), ALEKSEI KAZACHOK/SS; 129 (CTR RT), ANIKO GERENDI ENDERLE/SS; 129 (LO LE), ANIKO GERENDI ENDERLE/SS; 129 (FOOD), TALIZORA/SS; 130 (LE), NELIK/SS; 131 (UP CTR), TALIZORA/SS; 131 (UP RT), TRUDIE DAVIDSON/SS; 132 (ANTS), LIDIIA/SS; 133 (UP RT), DANIEL PRUDEK/SS; 134 (UP RT), ISSELEE/DREAMSTIME; 134 (LO LE), SEVENKE/SS; 134 (LO CTR), TALIZORA/SS; 135 (LO RT), MARTIAPUNTS/SS; 136-137 (BEAKERS), PUKACH/SS; 136-137 (ILLUSTRATIONS), MODUZA DESIGN; 138 (LE), PANDAWILD/SS; 138 (CTR RT), KIEV.VICTOR/SS; 138 (LO RT), KIEV.VICTOR/SS; 139 (UP LE), ERIC ISSELEE/SS; 139 (UP RT), YUNA_YUNA/SS; 140 (UP LE), VALENTYNA CHUKHLYEBOVA/SS; 140 (UP CTR), TALIZORA/SS; 140 (UP RT), NATURESMOMENTSUK/SS; 140 (LO RT), ALEKSEJS CUCKOVS/SS; 142 (CTR RT), TALIZORA/SS; 143 (CTR RT), TALIZORA/SS; 148 (COINS), STILLFX/SS; 153 (KITTEN), TOP PHOTO ENGINEER/SS; 154 (STREAM), TAKAHASHI_4/SS; 154 (WHITE HOUSE), TURTIX/SS

CREDITS

For the hippocampus: May it never be forgotten. —S. W. D.
For Theo, my wonderful little boy. —G. M.

Copyright © 2018 National Geographic Partners, LLC

Published by National Geographic Partners, LLC. All rights reserved. Reproduction of the whole or any part of the contents without written permission from the publisher is prohibited.

Since 1888, the National Geographic Society has funded more than 12,000 research, exploration, and preservation projects around the world. The Society receives funds from National Geographic Partners, LLC, funded in part by your purchase. A portion of the proceeds from this book supports this vital work. To learn more, visit natgeo.com/info.

NATIONAL GEOGRAPHIC and Yellow Border Design are trademarks of the National Geographic Society, used under license.

For more information, visit nationalgeographic.com, call 1-877-873-6864, or write to the following address:

National Geographic Partners
1145 17th Street N.W.
Washington, D.C. 20036-4688 U.S.A.

Visit us online at nationalgeographic.com/books

For librarians and teachers: ngchildrensbooks.org

More for kids from National Geographic: natgeokids.com

For information about special discounts for bulk purchases, please contact National Geographic Books Special Sales: specialsales@natgeo.com

For rights or permissions inquiries, please contact National Geographic Books Subsidiary Rights: bookrights@natgeo.com

Designed by Rachael Hamm Plett, Moduza Design

National Geographic supports K–12 educators with ELA Common Core Resources. Visit natgeoed.org/commoncore for more information.

Trade paperback ISBN: 978-1-4263-3017-9

The publisher would like to acknowledge the following people for making this book possible: Becky Baines, executive editor; Jen Agresta, project editor; Stephanie Warren Drimmer, narrative text author; Dr. Gareth Moore, puzzle creator and puzzle text author; Eva Absher-Schantz, art director; Rachael Hamm Plett, designer; Sarah J. Mock, photo editor; Michaela Weglinski, editorial assistant; Joan Gossett, editorial production manager; Molly Reid, production editor; Anne LeongSon and Gus Tello, design production assistants.

Printed in China
20/RRDH/3